Marian Pallister has worked [as a journalist and com]mentator, covering social iss[ues at home and around the] world, particularly in disaste[r zones. She has] taught journalism at Napier U[niversity and lectures] in English subjects at Argyll College. She also founded the Mthunzi and Lilanda Initiative, now known as ZamScotEd, a charity which supports the education of vulnerable young people in Zambia. Her previous books include *Lost Argyll*, *Argyll Curiosities*, *Cruachan: The Hollow Mountain* and *Yesterday Was Summer: The Marion Campbell Story*.

THE CRINAN CANAL

Marian Pallister

BIRLINN

First published in 2016 by
Birlinn Limited
West Newington House
10 Newington Road
Edinburgh
EH9 1QS

www.birlinn.co.uk

Copyright © Marian Pallister 2016

The moral right of Marian Pallister to be identified as the
author of this work has been asserted by her in accordance
with the Copyright, Designs and Patents Act 1988.

All rights reserved.
No part of this publication may be reproduced,
stored or transmitted in any form without the express
written permission of the publisher.

ISBN: 978 1 78027 346 4

British Library Cataloguing-in-Publication Data
A catalogue record for this book is available from the British Library

Typeset by Initial Typesetting Services, Edinburgh
Printed and bound by Grafica Veneta
(www.graficaveneta.com)

Contents

List of Illustrations	vii
An introduction	1
1. Choosing a site	13
2. An idea has its day	25
3. The drama begins	35
4. The cost of pozzolana and other inconveniences of war	47
5. The want of a nail	59
6. The disasters that had been waiting to happen	73
7. The fruits of incompetence	85
8. Towards a takeover	95
9. Rescue, disaster and rescue again	103
10. New beginnings, old problems	118
11. Not quite full steam ahead	142
12. Famine, feast and flower girls	151
13. Towards the *Linnet* years	164
14. The Royal Route takes off	180

15. Into the twentieth century and more plans for change	190
16. Sink or swim?	208
17. Very definitely swimming	218
A technical epilogue	223
Acknowledgements	229
Bibliography	231
Index	235

List of Illustrations

1. George Langland's map of the canal route, 1794.
2. Early 1790s elevation of the Bellanoch section of the Crinan Canal.
3. Early 1790s elevation of the Craiglass section of the Crinan Canal.
4. The entrance to the canal at Ardrishaig.
5. The troublesome locks, 11 and 12, at Dunardry.
6. The Dell section of the canal, drawn by John Rennie in 1792.
7. Early 1790s elevation showing planned rock-cutting.
8. The Crinan section of John Rennie's 1792 map.
9. Fishing skiff at Ardrishaig.
10. Ardrishaig pier.
11. The 'Royal Route' put the Crinan Canal on the map.
12. Thousands of passengers were disgorged from steamers landing from the Clyde.
13. As steam power grew in popularity, the canal suffered: it was too small for such boats.
14. The much-loved *Linnet* on the Crinan Canal.

15. The *Linnet* at Lock 9.
16. Bellanoch soon became a bustling village, thanks to the canal.
17. The Crinan Hotel.
18. The Glendarroch Distillery.
19. Towpaths were used to herd sheep and cattle to market.
20. Trading and fishing vessels were the canal's lifeblood.
21. The stances at Ardrishaig.
22. The prisoner-of-war camp at Cairnbaan.
23. Loch Fyne became a practice zone for the Normandy landings – the canal saw submarine traffic as a result.
24. Admiralty telegram requesting that navigation lights be extinguished during the blackout.
25. Lock gates at the Crinan Canal leading to the open sea.
26. The canal is routinely drained for maintenance.
27. The 'most beautiful shortcut in the world'.
28. Forestry paths offer a unique vista of the canal.
29. The River Add flows across Crinan Moss into Loch Crinan.

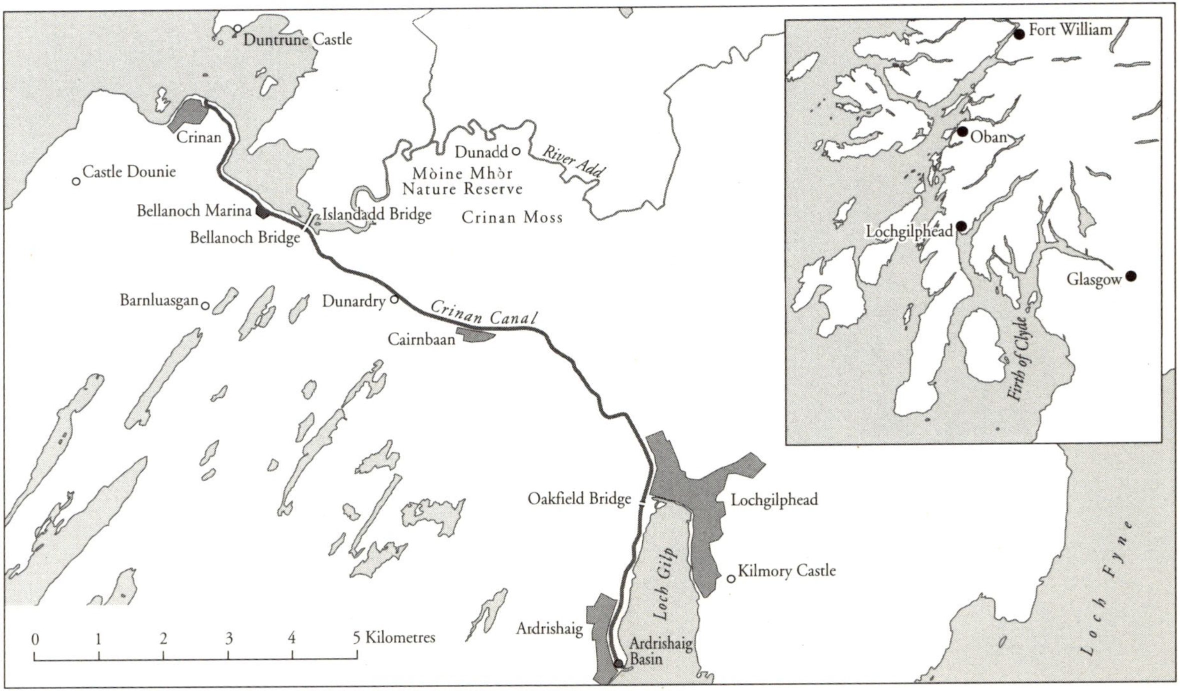

Duntrune Castle
Crinan
Castle Dounie
Bellanoch Marina
Islandadd Bridge
Bellanoch Bridge
Dunadd
River Add
Mòine Mhòr
Nature Reserve
Crinan Moss
Barnluasgan
Dunardry
Crinan Canal
Cairnbaan
Oakfield Bridge
Lochgilphead
Kilmory Castle
Loch Gilp
Ardrishaig
Ardrishaig
Basin
Loch Fyne
0
1
2
3
4
5 Kilometres
Fort William
Oban
Lochgilphead
Glasgow
Firth of Clyde

An introduction

If looks were everything, the Crinan Canal would be the only star of this show. Every inch of her sinuous nine miles offers a stunning view. From the entrance harbour at Ardrishaig to the exit into the sea at Crinan, this stretch of water linking Loch Fyne to the Atlantic has inspired paintings and photographs and is considered one of the most beautiful waterways in Britain – indeed, the 'most beautiful shortcut in the world'. The canal is of course the heroine of this story, and not just because she is a pretty face. She was to be an investment in the security of Hanoverian Great Britain and the safety of Argyll's fishermen, and in theory promised fortune for all who subscribed to her construction. She became a twinkle in the eye of her creators just two decades after Charles Stuart and his army were defeated at Culloden, and there was a lengthy cast list of people in high places who thought that a route across this particular finger of Argyll would be a good idea.

John, 5th Duke of Argyll, was one of the main marriage brokers who brought about the union of minds that conceived the plan to create a Highland version of the cutting-edge mode of transport that was beginning to sweep the whole of the British Isles. In a country without an infrastructure, creating waterways seemed the way to go. It was the duke, with Lord Breadalbane, who headed the lengthy list of subscribers buying into a project that at the time seemed guaranteed to be profitable. Like his predecessors, his was a major voice in Scottish politics. Born in 1723, 16 years after the Union of the Scottish and English parliaments, he had fought in Flanders during the War of Austrian Succession. He led a regiment opposing the Jacobites at Loch Fyne and later at the Battle of Falkirk and then Culloden. He laid aside his sword to become a Member of Parliament in London, spending time at his seat in Inveraray when possible. His knowledge not only of the Highland temperament that had led to rebellion but of the poverty and isolation experienced in the Highlands and Islands meant that his investment in a canal was not solely for his own personal gain. Of course his estates could be more financially viable with access to wider markets – but the exposure of fishermen and crofters to a wider world could only benefit and bring stability to the population and the country itself. This was still a time for 'taming' the Highlander.

Another of those most influential of men who sought to bring about the creation of the canal was Charles Schaw, ninth Baron Cathcart. A giant on the stage of the second half of the eighteenth century, he was a Lord of the Bedchamber. Like the Duke of Argyll, he had fought in the Austrian War of Succession. He had been HRH the Duke of Cumberland's aide-de-camp at the battle of Fontenoy in 1745, where he was shot in the face – Joshua Reynolds' portrait of him shows a black silk patch disguising the wound on an otherwise handsome, affable visage. The following year he fought on the winning side at Culloden. Cathcart had two periods as high commissioner of the General Assembly of the Church of Scotland and was Lord Commissioner of Police in Scotland, serving from 1764 to 1768. The Board of Police had been set up in 1714 and was financed by the English Treasury.

The aims were in effect to 'civilise' Scotland by appointing the right people in the Church, repairing roads, quelling unrest in the Highlands and improving exports. By the time Cathcart was appointed, the job was not as front-line as in the immediate aftermath of the 1715 and '45 Risings, but certain aspects still had to be addressed very seriously. Although it was after his return from Russia, where he was Ambassador to the Court of St Petersburg from 1768 to 1771, that he began to actively promote the creation of canals in Scotland, he had been in correspondence with Dougald (*sic*) MacTavish of Dunardry, one of the Argyll lairds, in the early 1760s.

He wrote to MacTavish in 1764: 'I have seen your letter to Mr Freebairn and a Sketch he had taken (without Instruments) of the ground lying betwixt the Lochs Crinan and Gilp, at your Desire.'

He had met with MacTavish in Inveraray and discussed the possibility of a canal, and now, having seen this survey by Mr Freebairn, he instructed a man named William Morris, son of the renowned Welsh marine surveyor Lewis Morris, to take 'an actual Survey' of the land between the two lochs, and also to the south between East and West Loch Tarbert.

Cathcart told MacTavish: 'The advantages to the Highlands from either Communication are obvious, but if a Passage could be gained sufficient for Herring Busses, the additional advantage that important Branch of the Fisheries would receive ought to be a further inducement.'

It wasn't all about helping the fishermen, of course. In the small world that was Scotland in the late eighteenth century, Lord Cathcart and Charles Freebairn were not strangers, and Mr Freebairn certainly has at least a walk-on part in our story. He described himself as an Edinburgh architect (though evidence of his work in that field is scant) and he was a man with interests in mineral mines in the Ochil Hills, on Loch Fyne and in Islay. In 1762, he had gone into business with a man called James Wright of Loss and the pair rented the Logie mines in the Stirling area that weren't entirely successful, although silver was present in the copper that was hewn.

According to John G. Harrison in his report *Heavy Metal Mines in the Ochil Hills: Chronology and Context*, Freebairn was a man with technical knowledge of the mineral mining process and he both invested his own capital and was involved in a practical sense too. Little wonder, then, that he was anxious to push the idea of a canal in Central Scotland (a canal was proposed to run from Dollar to Cambus on the Forth but didn't get off the drawing board), and one that would offer a less perilous journey from Islay (where in 1765 he boasted of great progress in his mineral mines) to the Clyde than the route round the hazardous Mull of Kintyre. In one of his letters to MacTavish of Dunardry, written on 13 February 1765, he expounded his grandiose plans for Islay, which included setting up furnaces, and confided (perhaps boasted):

> I have been instrumentall in fixing a plan of Navigation on the Devon as a favourable introduction to Inland communication in this Country for which purpose the Bill is now in Parliament at the instance of your friend Ld. Cathcart who will begin it the moment the Bill is passed. And I shall not faill to keep alive the Crinan Scheme and am in hopes his Lord[p] will visit it in Person once this summer and if possible I will accompany him.

Lord Cathcart was very evidently a forward thinker, and

possibly it was his posting to the Russian court that made him put the canal ideas on the backburner for a few years. But he wasn't alone in working towards some development of transport and of ways to improve the fishing industry.

Pamphlets and essays were being circulated around this period, including those of the influential philanthropist John Knox. Action, however, was painfully slow and it wasn't until 1778 that 25 Scottish movers and shakers got together in London and set up the Highland Society of London to bring about this sort of improvement to the Highlands, as well as to support Highlanders adrift in London. It very quickly became an august and robust organisation (it brought about the end of the proscription of tartan imposed after the '45 Rising, suggesting its members felt that winning hearts and minds was preferable to crushing culture and killing clan rebels).

John Knox was invited to address the Society and, in part, was responsible for plans for the Crinan Canal going ahead; Knox is another important figure who shaped its earliest days. He is so often overlooked in favour of his austere sixteenth-century namesake, and yet much of modern Scotland stems from the work he carried out in his retirement. Born in Dalkeith in 1720, he spent much of his life in London running a bookshop. When he retired, with money in the bank, he went home to Scotland and in 1764, the year Cathcart had been in touch with MacTavish of Dunardry, began a series of visits that shocked him to the core. The poverty he saw throughout the Highlands led to him writing a number of very influential publications and to that invitation to speak to the Highland Society of London. He didn't go in for catchy titles, but *A View of the British Empire, more especially Scotland, with some Proposals for the Improvement of that Country, the Extension of its Fisheries, and the Relief of the People,* which was published in 1784, ran to several editions and did exactly what its title implies. His most important suggestions included canals between the Forth and Clyde, Loch Fyne and the Atlantic, and Fort William and Inverness.

Hand in hand with these proposals went his scheme for creating up to 50 fishing villages in the Highlands. This was the idea he presented to the Highland Society of London and it was later published, again with a less than captivating title but with content that set the heather on fire: *A discourse on the expediency of establishing fishing stations: or small towns, in the Highlands of Scotland and the Hebride Islands* (1786). British Fisheries came out of this flurry of innovative thought (known initially as the British Society for Extending the Fisheries and Improving the Sea Coast of this Kingdom). It was set up with a capital of £150,000, and the Duke of Argyll was appointed its governor.

Fishing and the creation of the Crinan Canal are, of course, inextricably linked. The herring industry provided a living for the people of Loch Fyne, one of Scotland's longest sea lochs – but to fish beyond its 40-mile stretch meant navigating the Mull of Kintyre. Fierce, unpredictable weather and strong currents still make this a challenging voyage, but in the eighteenth century the small craft that existed made it extraordinarily dangerous. The suggestion to build a canal, which with the help of John Knox eventually made its appearance in Westminster, was sound commercial sense – and would also create a life-saving route to the Atlantic fishing grounds.

With a plan backed by Scotland's great and good on the table, this 'cast list' can begin to include names that we know today as titans in the world of engineering. It is important to remember, however, that at the time tentative plans for the Crinan Canal were being made, these men were just beginning to make their way in the world. And the world in the final decades of the eighteenth century seems very small indeed compared with our own. Although very structured in a class sense, connections were able to be made that today would seem improbable.

Lord Cathcart, that major player in the early days of our story, inherited estates in Greenock from his mother Marion Schaw and sold the family estate of Sundrum to James Murray of Broughton in 1758. The Greenock estates brought him into the company of a man named James Watt, a shipwright famous for making precision instruments, who at one stage in his career employed 14 men but was by now reduced in circumstances after the loss of a valuable ship. Mr Watt was involved in the Church of Scotland in Greenock. Cathcart signed over some land on which Watt built a church, and additional lands for public works.

This link of course takes us to another vital player in this story – one whose name is always at the forefront of any history of the Crinan Canal. James Watt Junior made an official survey in 1771, commissioned by Cathcart. James Watt Senior had evidently provided useful information ahead of this survey because Cathcart's instructions to his acquaintance's son read: 'I beg you will thank your father from me for his dispatch relating to Tarbert & Creinan Passages and tell him these things will be examined.'

James Watt's survey may have been the deciding factor in choosing the Crinan route over the Tarbert route, but in many ways he was also the author of our beautiful heroine's downfall. At the time he made that very first survey in 1771, he was learning his craft as a surveyor. He'd been a sickly boy and to an extent relied on the drawing his mother had taught him and the maths he was already absorbing as a child of six. There is a story that his aunt wrote him off as an 'idle boy' because he spent hours taking the lid on and off the kettle, watching the steam rise from the spout and catching the drops of water. 'Are you not ashamed of spending your time this way?' she asked the boy – but of course, she was not to know that this would be James Watt of steam-engine fame. His development of steam power (which led to the world's first steam vessel, PS *Comet*, being launched on the Clyde in 1812) brought boats that were not only too big for the canal's width and depth but also, in a very few years, powerful enough to make it round the Mull of Kintyre literally 'under their own steam'.

Watt was not the only glittering name to have started his career with a lowly role in the Crinan Canal's development. John Rennie is now regarded as the man whose waterways 'underpinned the industrial revolution', according to the Canal and River Trust. Born into a farming family near East Linton, some 20 miles from Edinburgh, in 1761, he was just a child when Watt first surveyed the site of the Crinan Canal – but a child already working with Andrew Meikle, the engineer responsible for inventing the threshing machine. Rennie continued his studies while working in this innovative environment, and graduated from Edinburgh University before going to work in Birmingham with a steam-engine company called Boulton and Watt.

Yes – that Watt. After that first survey for the Crinan Canal in 1771 James Watt's career developed quickly. From being an instrument maker, production engineer and merchant (and frankly, anything related that would raise an income), Watt turned his hand to chemical, civil and mechanical engineering. Life still was not too promising, but he decided in 1774 to move to Birmingham and it was there that his fortunes changed and he went into partnership with Matthew Boulton to develop the steam engine. This was an ideal firm for the young John Rennie. He met Watt in 1783, was offered a contract installing steam engines in some of the Boulton and Watt projects, and, having learned a trick or two, he moved to London and set up his own engineering business there in 1791. By the time parliament had passed an Act in 1793 allowing the Crinan Canal to be constructed, Rennie was already making a name working on the Lancaster Canal in England. This led to the job of designing and building the Crinan Canal. However, his work on the Rochdale and Lancaster Canals, his drainage work in the Fens, and then the Kennet and Avon Canal, a contract that lasted from 1794 to 1810, seem to have been his priorities.

Even when Rennie came back to Scotland to get the Crinan Canal project up and running in 1793, he was also contracted to build the bridge over the Water of Leith. He based himself in Leith and it seems that it was mainly his employees who spent time in Argyll on the job. One of those, described as a surveyor, was John Paterson, who had to be sent to England to see what a canal actually looked like before he took on the work of overseeing the building of the waterway between Loch Gilp and Loch Crinan. His name is not one that history has sprinkled with stardust, but his role was critical during the canal's chequered progress. Enough to say that, in the same way that St Paul's Cathedral is synonymous with the name Sir Christopher Wren (and we hope that the name of the late Enric Moralles will conjure up the Scottish Parliament 200 years from now), John Rennie and James Watt are names that cannot be separated from the Crinan Canal, while it would be better had Paterson never taken that crash course in canal construction.

Thomas Telford is also seen as a cornerstone of modern engineering. Yet another Scot, it was he who carried forward most of the plans to establish fishing villages, construct roads and build the canals advised by John Knox. And when things began to fall apart for the Crinan Canal, he was sent from the construction site of the Caledonian Canal to rescue the distressed project. Telford was by that time well known for efficient canals in England.

What few took into account when planning both roads and canals in the Scottish Highlands, however, was the very different terrain to be encountered and conquered. As we shall see, Rennie had confronted difficulties building canals in England, and Telford was born and bred in Eskdale and was also aware that Scotland was not the green and, in an engineering sense, biddable land known to the majority of those who subscribed to the building of the Crinan Canal. Telford was a realist. A canal, he said, was the working of a great machine, 'in the first place to draw money out of the pockets of numerous proprietary to make an expensive canal, and then to make the money return into their pockets by the creation of a business upon that canal'.

As the project gained momentum, there were people falling over each other to 'prove' that a canal between Loch Fyne and the Atlantic would put money back into the pockets of the investors. That was never to happen, and time after time the canal would be threatened with an ignominious end. The story should therefore include some minor figures who over the centuries helped to keep the waterway alive – characters as diverse as Queen Victoria and James Bond, the *Linnet* and the Dalriada Project (Victoria made a journey through the canal in the 1840s accompanied by children waving floral garlands; *Skyfall*, the 2012 Bond movie, was filmed in part at the western end of the canal; the *Linnet* was a plucky little steamer that carried thousands of visitors through the waterway for decades; and the Dalriada Project modernised the canal's walkways and signage, supported a written and aural twentieth-century history, and left as its legacy the Heart of Argyll Tourism Alliance).

While the history of the canal must mention landowners such as MacTavish and the Malcolms of Poltalloch, through whose lands the canal was built, there were also, of course, the workers, whose role is rarely documented. One important mention, that 400 men had 'already done wonders' by 1794, was recorded for posterity by Lachlan MacTavish in a letter to his friend Coll Lamont of Monydrain, a property around a third of the distance to Loch Crinan from the Loch Fyne side, beyond which the construction already reached when the letter was written.

More will be heard of these important individuals in the canal's history, and there would be other interesting and influential people who sought to improve, to change, even to close the canal. Some were geniuses, some were scoundrels, some were simply incompetent, and some didn't even know where this beautiful little canal was.

1

Choosing a site

There is an apocryphal Irish story that, asked for directions in his city, a Dubliner told the confused visitor, 'I wouldn't have started from here.' A twenty-first-century geologist, Dr Roger Anderton, has taken much the same approach to the Crinan Canal after exploring the nature of the composition of its route. It may indeed merit the sobriquet 'the most beautiful shortcut in the world', but had today's surveying instruments been available in the 1770s, these particular nine miles and two chains (nine miles and 44 yards) might never have been chosen to secure a safe passage to the Atlantic, an opening up of markets for the Highlands and Islands, and potential profit for investors. The Crinan Canal is the product of its time. Local landowners had their agenda, as did the government of the day. Few 'ordinary' people would be consulted in the planning process, but it was recognised that the dangers of fishermen could be diminished and that the market for commodities between the Islands and the Clyde could be increased. Although in the centuries ahead politicians would dismiss this canal as an unnecessary backwater, it was conceived, planned and built against the backdrop of world affairs. Its physical position was in part influenced by the continuing nervousness of a London government concerning the activities and allegiances of a Highland population and the increasing threat of European aggression.

With hindsight, the second half of the eighteenth century was the launch pad for modernity. The exact period of the Enlightenment is questioned – some claim it began in the 1620s and ended in the 1780s; for others it began in 1650 and ended in 1800. But surely there can be no pinning down with exactitude a period when throughout Western Europe philosophers and scholars turned the world of ideas on its head? It was a century when the 'individual' emerged and questioned authority. Cultural, intellectual and scientific ideas exploded like firecrackers across Western Europe, and Scotland shared with France a leading role in the whole exciting process. David Hume and Adam Smith are names known to us all, but in Scotland it was really scientific and medical thinking that led the world. Joseph Black, the physicist and chemist who died in 1799, discovered carbon dioxide (fixed air) and latent heat. He was just one of the contributors to British science who helped Scotland to punch well above its weight. Black opened up a whole new sphere to those who followed – including that key player in the development of the Crinan Canal, James Watt. This period led to industrialisation. Cottage industries became commercial concerns – inventor Richard Arkwright opened the first cotton mill in Derbyshire in 1771 – and although the 'factory age' did not progress smoothly (there were strikes and violence; machinery that didn't work as it was intended), progress it certainly did. And James Watt put scientific theory into practice, contributing disproportionately to the advance of mechanisation across the industrial landscape.

When Watt first surveyed the possible routes for the canal that would transform the lives of fishermen in Argyll, he was already using a basic form of theodolite that he had invented. His subsequent work was mainly concerned with steam power, used first to pump water from mines before being adapted to drive industrial machinery, propel ships and drive railway engines. Ironically, it was this facet of Watt's work that threatened the very existence of the canal that his early theodolite helped bring into being.

This placing of the canal's story against the backdrop of the Enlightenment and the Factory Age suggests a country already moving into the modern era. Not entirely so. Although Edinburgh has been called 'the Enlightenment in stone' and the New Town was created in the second half of the eighteenth century, most of Scotland was still grimly medieval, as Samuel Johnson was quick to point out in the account of his tour around the country in 1773 – the very year that Watt's official survey was published. Johnson's stay at an inn in Inveraray, Scotland's first planned new town, which was still in the process of construction, impressed him as few other inns or dwelling houses encountered on the journey had. Had he and James Boswell come across James Watt on their Scottish travels, Boswell would certainly not have bothered to record such a meeting. He much preferred to name-drop, referring to dining with the likes of the Duke of Argyll, who was in residence at the time of the Johnson/ Boswell Inveraray stop-over. Johnson's remarks about travel in Scotland often seem little short of deliberately insulting – but we have to accept that he seems to have told only the truth.

The population of the country was around 1.5 million, and as is the case today people were mostly massed in the Central Belt. The Highland Clearances had begun in the 1750s and populations in the Highlands and Islands had been dispersed to the cities or to the colonies. Leaving their homes was for most people difficult in every sense, not least the travel to their destinations. Samuel Smiles tells us in his *Life of Thomas Telford Civil Engineer with an Introductory History of Roads and Travelling in Great Britain* that in the mid-1700s 'the streets in the towns and the roads in the country were alike rude and wretched'. It took two weeks to reach London from Edinburgh by road, and coaches went once a month. There were highwaymen, but the greater danger was the conditions of the roads, which were narrow, muddy, and usually little better than bridle paths. Smiles could only say that the Highland routes migrant workers would have travelled were 'of course' still worse. If Shanks's pony is the only option for travel, mountain tracks may not have seemed so bad – the lack of paved roads impeded those who sought to travel on horseback or in carriages. When William and Dorothy Wordsworth travelled in Scotland with Samuel Taylor Coleridge in 1803, more than two decades after Watt made his first surveys for the Crinan Canal, Dorothy explained in her journal that the roads were so bad that '. . . it meant going most of the way by foot'.

There had been some very substantial and well-designed bridges and stretches of road built in Scotland in the Middle Ages, but only to facilitate the progress of the ruling classes. The flurry of road building in the wake of the 1715 and then 1745 Uprisings was designed to allow troops to move quickly to the source of trouble. By 1740 General George Wade, who was in charge of the operation, facilitated the building of 250 miles of substantial 16-foot-wide roads in Scotland, along with 40 bridges, having reported to the government in London that the lack of roads and bridges made it difficult to communicate between garrisons. Even so, in 1745 the lack of roads enabled the Highlanders to outstrip organised military forces. They were able to travel by mountain routes, while the roads were still inadequate for troops and only joined up the dots between garrisons. Creating a proper infrastructure in the Highlands became an imperative in the second half of the eighteenth century – the 'savages', as the Highlanders were consistently referred to, were still making the government a little jumpy.

The powers-that-be had tried retribution and now there was a growing idea that rehabilitation could be a better policy. Before the century was out, projects such as the Crinan Canal were being taken very seriously, and a main aim of a canal between Loch Fyne and the Atlantic was without doubt an intention to 'civilise the savages'. Certainly such a route would speed access to trouble spots. However, as the century progressed there was more concern for turning a profit than quelling uprisings, and John Knox's humanitarian ideas nicely sugar-coated the more hard-headed business motives of lairds, investors, mine owners and the budding entrepreneurs who envisaged that worldwide trading would be enabled by this little stretch of water.

The position of the canal was not, however, a certainty from the outset. The alternative considered – and surveyed by Watt – was the route between East and West Lochs Tarbert, around 15 miles to the south of the Loch Gilp-Loch Crinan possibility. It wasn't the first time that this route was presented as a crucial waterway. Legend tells us that when the Norse king Magnus Barefoot made a deal with Scotland about possession of territory, the terms were that he was to have all he could sail around. In 1098, he had his men drag a boat between West Loch Tarbert and East Loch Tarbert so that he could lay claim to Kintyre, as well as the Islands. This ingenious ploy showed that this was indeed a feasible route for a waterway.

There was strong lobbying in the late eighteenth century for this route and, to the layperson, its shorter length, the natural harbour within the East Loch and the sheltered exit towards the sea leading from the West Loch, would seem to suggest a cheaper and better option. Indeed, Watt's father was pushing for this route and almost lost Watt Junior the surveying job because there was suspicion of bias. Writing from Glasgow on 21 December 1772 to the Commissioners of Highland Roads and Bridges, Watt explained that in July 1771 he had surveyed both sites. His descriptions of each are extensive and very candid – he owns up to having little maritime knowledge – and he concludes with the advantages and disadvantages of each site.

For a Tarbert canal, among the advantages he noted that it would 'be a passage not only to the north, but also to the islands of Islay and Jura, with the external coast of Knapdale, the west side of Kantire [Kintyre]'. A Tarbert canal would have 'very safe harbours at both ends'; there was 'the shortness of the artificial navigation'; most locks could be cut from rock, so the expense would be less; there would be 'no deep cutting in very soft materials, unless at the summit . . .'; and with 'a great part of the canal being rock, it will require few repairs'. The downside was that the Tarbert route did not have 'a direct passage to the North Highlands, and that the direction of the West Loch being towards the south-west vessels may be detained in it when the wind is otherwise fair for them'. Similarly, winds could prevent vessels entering the West Loch 'when with the same wind they could easily have made their passage at Crinan'. Watt further explained: '. . . the West Loch is a long narrow passage in which vessels cannot conveniently tack, and that it is generally shallow near the shores and in its bays'. He added that at the summit of this route there wasn't 'a sufficient quantity of water' and it would have to be brought across rough ground from considerable distances. He was also uncertain how much it would cost for the 'great quantity of cutting in rock'. He gave equally fair reasons for and against the Loch Gilp-Loch Crinan route, and the costings he estimated for a canal seven feet in depth were £34,879.0s.4d at Crinan and £17,988.10s.6d at Tarbert; and for ten feet in depth, £48,405.5s.3d at Crinan and £23,883.7s at Tarbert.

Watt perhaps had a finger in too many pies, as he struggled to make ends meet in those early days before his move to Birmingham, his partnership with Boulton and his success with steam. The surveys at Tarbert and between Loch Gilp and Loch Crinan were completed at the end of July 1771. He left Tarbert to return to Glasgow on 31 July. Apparently the weather was bad and a meeting with his friend, Charles 'Crichan' MacDowall, to survey for a canal from Drumlemble to Campbeltown was postponed. MacDowall was an advocate, sometime Sheriff of Renfrewshire, and by 1771 the new owner of the lease on the Duke of Argyll's Campbeltown coal and salt works. He pursued Watt throughout the autumn of that year to make the journey to Campbeltown to carry out his survey, but it was not until 8 June 1773 that Watt actually went to carry out the work. MacDowall may have been patient because this was a friend, or because he rated him highly as a surveyor. There are other references to Watt taking his time to carry out or complete contracts, and modern commentaries suggest that he may have been deliberately negligent.

However, it is more likely that this was simply a man of his time. No objections are recorded about the delay between that July 1771 survey and the detailed letter sent by Watt

17 months later on 21 December 1772 to the Commissioners of Highland Roads and Bridges. Correspondence between many of the players in this story shows a lack of urgency alien to the twenty-first century but evidently perfectly acceptable in the late eighteenth century. It took another 20 years before the project was actually started, and while there is evidence of lobbying for it to proceed, the time lapse seems to have caused none of the indignant protest we would have witnessed today.

There were, of course, other things concerning both local heritors and politicians. On 16 December 1773, the Boston Tea Party saw violent protest against the policies of the British government when a shipment of tea was tipped into Boston harbour. This was an act of defiance against taxes imposed by a government in which colonists had no representation. The responses of the British government over the next two years led to armed conflict between Britain and the 13 American states that had declared independence. The American War of Independence, fought from 1775 to 1783, not only required finance and troops but led to increased friction between Britain and the French, who were still miffed at having lost the Seven Years War. Spain and the Netherlands joined in the fray. By the time John Rennie moved to London in 1785, Samuel Smiles suggests in his *Lives of the Engineers: Smeaton and Rennie* that the country was 'in a state of serious depression in consequence of the unsuccessful termination of the American War'.

As always after such a period of expense (and let us not forget the succession of other skirmishes that Britain had been involved in for the best part of the century) government debt was high and taxes rose to meet it. There were some apparent positives on the horizon (the India Bill renewed by William Pitt the Younger, the country's youngest-ever prime minister

CHOOSING A SITE 21

on his election in 1783, kick-started the boom in trade with the sub-continent) but a trade treaty with France fell through when the Revolution began there. The Revolution, of course, brought political upheaval spilling across Europe and threatening Britain from 1788 to 1799. With no time to draw breath, from 1799 to 1815 the Napoleonic Wars continued the menace to our coastlines and made demands on British resources. To add to this confusion, the Irish rebelled against Britain in 1798 and were aided by a faction from France.

There were genuine fears that the country could be invaded, and throughout Argyll men were recruited as a force to ward off attack as part of recently instituted Scottish and local militias. Robert Burns was called up to the Royal Dumfries Volunteers. When he died in 1796, he was given a military funeral, and a cocked hat and his sword were placed on the coffin. What a pity we could not hear the poem that resulted from that. The Argylshire [sic] Fencible Regiment was of course under the command of Inveraray Castle. Argyll men were not just on stand-by in case of invasion: they were sent to quell rebels in Ireland and even served in Gibraltar. Burns may have been given a cocked hat, but the Argyll men's uniforms were often unfit for purpose but purposely improved to keep the troops on side. In an attempt to regularise these *Dad's Army* soldiers, the system of Lords Lieutenant of the county was established.

As a result of this rash of conflicts across Europe, the building of the canal, once begun, was hampered by lack of appropriate building materials. The right sort of cement for underwater work, for example, could not be imported from Italy. With the Crinan entrance to the canal viewed as particularly vulnerable to penetration by French troops, there was an atmosphere of nervousness among those charged with the safety of the western seaboard of Scotland. Letters between the Duke of Argyll and Mid Argyll landowner Neill Malcolm suggest tensions were very real. It was not necessarily articulated in correspondence, but this was not just about a foreign invasion. The sixth verse of the anthem written after 1745 (which, of course, became the British national anthem) specified:

> Lord grant that Marshal Wade
> May by thy mighty aid
> Victory bring.
> May he sedition hush,
> And like a torrent rush,
> Rebellious Scots to crush.
> God save the King!

The fear must still have been palpable that the 'rebellious Scots' might again need to be crushed.

There were also very practical reasons why this site was chosen for the canal, but nowhere could offer an ideal situation. Although Tarbert had been cited as having difficulties in terms of an easy provision of water for a canal there, the lochans in the hills above the Crinan location did not have a consistent supply either. As we shall see, the system of supplying water to the canal would prove one of the major problems in terms of its construction and maintenance, and those problems link to an additional element that would plague the canal throughout its history: the weather. Argyll is a lush, green county. A generous rainfall and the warmth of the Gulf Stream maintain that lushness. While climate chaos has undoubtedly increased at an alarming rate throughout the industrial era, there have always been blips in temperature and rainfall – the exception so often proves the rule. Sometimes those lochans were dangerously low in water; more often they threatened to overflow. *The First Statistical Accounts of Scotland* were collated in the 1790s. From the parishes bordering to the north of the line of the proposed canal, the Revd Mr Hugh Campbell said in his account of Kilmartin that the climate, 'although wet, is not unhealthy', while the Revd Mr Dugald Campbell, minister of the neighbouring Glassary, referred to 'wet seasons' in the way that African countries refer to their 'rainy seasons'. He said: 'The air is generally moist, and the climate rainy, which renders farming here very precarious, and often unprofitable.' The Revd Mr Archibald Campbell in North Knapdale parish, south of the canal line, could only agree that the climate was 'rainy'. In times when 'rainy' became 'deluge', the lochans and waterfalls that had been identified by Watt as so much more accessible than possible water supplies to a potential Tarbert canal were to cause disastrous damage to the nascent Crinan Canal.

Rennie had experienced working on the Lancaster waterway when seven acres of land slid into the canal site and forced its way into the valley below. The system of small tunnels and intercepting drains that were then cut into the hillside to prevent a recurrence was certainly successful – but costly. The Crinan project budget would always be tight and innovative measures never quite seemed to live up to expectations.

It is interesting, however, that even as the first sods were turned to construct the Crinan Canal, when it must have been the talk of every household that a large squad of men were moving in to create a waterway that promised to revolutionise fishing, trade and life itself, the Revd Mr Campbell in Kilmartin included his own parish to the north of the canal line in a general and unenthusiastic introduction to his report for *The First Statistical Account*. He wrote: 'Remote Highland parishes, distant from the scenes of great and memorable events, backward in most kinds of improvements, particularly in agriculture, and without trade or manufactures, cannot be expected to furnish much material for statistical inquiry.' But then, Mr Campbell was the minister who also wrote that there was nothing of interest in his parish of an archaeological or historical nature. This in a glen overflowing with monoliths and burial cairns that today attract as many tourists as does the canal that was then being built on the boundaries of his parish to improve trade.

If Mr Campbell was a man with his eyes closed, there were plenty around him taking advantage of this time of innovation, change, progress and war. It is perhaps ironic that during the era of the French Revolutionary and Napoleonic wars, from 1793 to 1815, the precarious international situation actually created prosperity, optimism and economic growth in the Highlands. There are always entrepreneurs who will profit from a war. Burning seaweed may not have brought in a 'living wage', as we think of it today, to those who actually did the job, but the kelping industry flourished as landowners sought alternatives to increasingly inaccessible imported fertilisers. The new fishing villages got under way. And as much for protection as development, the new infrastructure of Scotland was begun. The Crinan Canal was part of that economic growth.

2

An idea has its day

James Watt had come out in favour of the Crinan route. Two decades later, John Rennie agreed and prepared plans, and a prospectus was put together to sell subscriptions to make this canal a viable – no, profitable – project. A letter from the MacTavish of Dunardry papers held in the archives at Lochgilphead describes that prospectus as 'indeed . . . as well done as could be from general observation'. Headed 'Prospectus of the Advantages to be derived from the Crinan Canal', this all-important document was boldly rhetorical in its introduction. It declares:

> The important advantage which would result to the inhabitants of the western and north-west coasts of Scotland and to the commerce and fisheries of those parts of the kingdom . . . are so obvious and so generally acknowledged, that it is almost unnecessary to enumerate them.

A description of the horrors of the 'Mull of Cantire' concludes with another less than objective statement that the danger proffered by the peninsula 'is justly considered as one of the principal hindrance to the extension of the fisheries, and one great cause of the distresses of the people of these countries'.

The plight of people in the Highlands and Islands, cut off as they were from major towns and with no infrastructure to progress any industry, was cited in the prospectus in a way that avoided any of the demonising that had followed 1745. Further persuasive rhetoric (who wants to be called a 'superficial observer' and who would admit to being one of the 'ignorant'?) cast aside all the previous stereotyping:

> Superficial observers, ignorant of the difficulties attendant on insular life, and the peculiar circumstances of the people in those islands, too frequently impute to them indolence and supineness of disposition. On the contrary, acute, intrepid, and hardy, there is no set of men more assiduous and alert in seizing the opportunities of industry presented to them, and their efforts to overcome the natural obstacles of their situation, in many cases, are much to be admired.

The canal itself was presented as a waterway almost as important and as grand as the one built by Darius I of Persia in the sixth century BC to link the Nile and the Red Sea (a precursor of the Suez Canal that would be planned in the mid-nineteenth century). It wouldn't only serve the fishermen and islanders, but vessels coming from Liverpool and Bristol 'and other parts of the west coasts of England and east coast of Ireland' that had trade with the Baltic, and 'even vessels to the West Indies from the Clyde, will in some cases prefer this passage, if built to draw less water, or by the slip keel'. There is an almost devious persuasiveness in the language of the prospectus. In the same paragraph that the possibilities of such increased trading are dangled before prospective subscribers, their better natures are also appealed to: 'The inestimable benefit which must arise therefrom to the inhabitant...are extremely interesting to a benevolent mind, and may alone be an inducement to many to subscribe without an anxious regard to future profit.' That ten members of the clergy (including three from the same family – the Revd Arthur Homer, Magdalen College, Oxford; the Revd William Homer and the Revd Philip Homer) signed up to invest in the Crinan Canal becomes easier to understand in the light of such moral coercion.

There follows much about the deprivations that the local inhabitants suffered – their lack of salt, the fact that they might not be able to gather enough peats to warm themselves – and this is counterbalanced by the solutions: vessels from the Clyde could take salt, coal and other commodities to the Islands through this new waterway at no cost to their safety. Changes in the excise duties could be made to make this a profitable venture ('. . . it might be expected that the indulgence of government would allow coals to pass through the canal free from duty, which would be an inestimable privilege, and soon render the inhabitants able to bear a full proportion of other taxes'). We can hear the subtleties of modern politics in play here – 'get them into work and they'll be able to contribute to the economy like the rest of us' is a sub-text that plays alongside the sympathy card and the 'get-rich-quick' hints. This is a truly remarkable document, but has more than a little in common with a twenty-first-century shady estate agent's description of a garret bedsit as 'bijou residence with huge potential'. The Glasgow 'neighbours' with whom the canal would allow mutual trading are praised as 'intelligent'; and the resulting 'comfort and happiness' would prevent more migration from the Highlands and Islands to the colonies (ironic, then, that sailing from Crinan to America was commemorated in Gaelic song in the nineteenth century).

There was, it was pointed out, no government help for building canals in England and it was considered best that none would be sought for this project – that subscriptions should meet the costs. Being involved in a venture that would bring 'so many public and national advantages' (including a rise in the value of land, the prospectus suggested) was a major incentive, and the project should (but no promises) yield a 'reasonable interest'. Rather coyly, the prospectus refers to 'two noblemen, highly distinguished for their public spirit', who had recently commissioned a major survey 'by an eminent engineer' to determine the best line for the canal and the 'probable' expense. Note the language that makes no firm promises when it says: 'By their report, *it appears* that a canal can be made of sufficient depth for large vessels, with a plentiful supply of water, and at a moderate expense.' (The italics are those of this author.)

The prospectus recorded meetings that had been held in London in June of 1792, and on 16 October 1792 at Inveraray. Notices required by the rules of the House of Commons had been published, resolutions unanimously taken, and 'a subscription begun for the making of the canal'. This document was therefore aimed at a wider audience, clearly to ensure that there would be sufficient money in the kitty to meet one or other of John Rennie's two plans (for it was he, of course, who was the 'eminent engineer'). The document claimed:

> in order to second the endeavours of the noblemen [the Duke of Argyll and Lord Breadalbane] and gentlemen who are desirous of promoting the subscription, this statement has been drawn up, and it now remains to give as correct an account as could be obtained of the trade likely to pass through the canal and the probable produce of lockage dues.

The 'market research' that had been carried out suggested that because of the time savings the route would create (and no doubt there were those who also factored in that fewer vessels would be smashed up on the rocks of the Mull of 'Cantire' and fewer lives lost), companies would be willing to pay 1s 6d per ton to pass through the canal. It is difficult to give that sum a perspective in terms of value today, because of inflation, but in 1792, a private soldier in the regular infantry was paid £9.2s.6d a year, and a commander in the navy was paid 20 shillings a day. However, the proprietors of the canal set out to appear generous. According to the Commissioners of the Customs, the estimated annual tonnage sailing from the Clyde to the Western Isles was 43,600 tons. Calculating that each of these vessels would pass through the canal at least once in a voyage, charging one shilling would bring in £2,180. It was calculated that even if only a third of the vessels used the canal, there would still be a decent profit. Why be greedy, especially if the Baltic trade, averaging 16,992 tons annually from 1789 to 1792, could be persuaded to sail through the new waterway?

There was also an expectation that fishing would be extended – boats from all of the Clyde ports could be expected to head out to the Atlantic by the new route if it allowed them access to a wider range of fish. There were 1,000 open boats in the Firth of Clyde and, the prospectus hazarded, more than twice that number in the whole of the Islands and coast heading north from Crinan. If each averaged four tons and each paid four shillings per boat for one voyage through the canal, that would be £400 in the pockets of the subscribers.

The list of cargoes that could be traded through this little miracle channel included kelp, of which at that time 7,000 tons were produced annually (and the international situation that would worsen in coming years made this even more valuable, but there was no crystal ball involved in the writing of this prospectus, only healthy exaggeration). There were also slates, marble, quartz sand, limestone and shell sand, lead and lead ore and other minerals. The kelp, sand and limestone would be made into fertilisers for agricultural land across Scotland. The Highland Society of London was in the process of promoting the improvement of agriculture in Scotland, in part based on a report by the late Dr Walker, a professor of natural history at Edinburgh University, who had left a report entitled 'An Economical History of the Highlands' for which the society had made a grant of £20. The late Dr Smith of 'Campbelton' had produced an agricultural survey of the Hebrides, for which the society also made available a grant of £20. Landowners in Scotland, including Neill Malcolm and, of course, the Duke of Argyll, were also attempting to bring farming into the eighteenth century, even as it was fast coming to a close. The slates would come from Easdale, Ballachuilish and Appin; the marble from Tiree, Iona and Nether Lorne. Already the marble was a 'must-have' in public buildings and private houses of style in London, Bath and Leith. These lands to the north and west of the canal owned by the 'two noblemen, highly distinguished for their public spirit', cousins Lord Breadalbane and the Duke of Argyll, were the source of all these valuable commodities, so perhaps as well as their undoubted public spirit there was just a degree of self-interest.

The prospectus noted that although the cost of the canal would be high, there would obviously be an economy of scale: the more subscribers there were, the lower the cost to each individual, and if the work were to be 'carried on with judgement, economy and despatch, the canal may, in a very short space of time, be opened for the passage of vessels, and will yield a return to subscribers every year, increasing with the wealth and population which must be its necessary consequence'.

John Rennie had submitted two estimates, each for a different route. One he called 'Dell Passage' and the other 'Achinshelloch Passage'. (Achnashelloch is the modern spelling.) Each of these began at Ardrishaig in Loch Gilp (an inlet of Loch Fyne). The 'Dell Passage' terminated in the Bay of Crinan in ten feet of water at low tides. It was the shorter route by two miles. The 'Achinshelloch Passage' terminated at the Point of Duntroon (or Duntrune) on the north side of Loch Crinan near the Malcolm family's castle, with its thirteenth-century origins. The summit of the 'Dell' route would be higher, a harbour would have to be built at Crinan, and the course of the River Add itself would have to be altered to accommodate the shorter route. The cost for 'Dell' was calculated at £63,628.11s. The Achinshelloch costing was £62,456.11s. Another point in its favour was that Rennie did not expect the harbour to become 'choked up'. Despite all of this and the potential £1,172 saving, the so-called 'Dell Passage' won out.

The optimism was palpable. On 8 February 1793, James Maxwell of Aros in Mull exuded that confidence when he wrote to his friend Lachlan MacTavish at his place of employment in the tax office in Edinburgh, knowing of his interest in the proposed canal because the traditional MacTavish family seat at Dunardry would very soon be on the very banks of the Crinan Canal:

The expedition with which the subscription to the Crinan Canal has been compleated [*sic*] exceeded the most sanguine expectations of every body, and I think must have given a fine fillip to the Duke's health and spirits, as it was a matter that he so much interested himself in and had so greatly at heart. [The duke was 70 years old in 1793.]

Mr Maxwell's own excitement must have been quite catching. He told MacTavish:

> In the course of a year or two I do not despair of being able to set out in the morning from Mull with a cargo of Braxy mutton, shot lambs and skins and arrive at a ready market for them in Greenock before night.

Tellingly, he added:

> I must confess however that I expect the revenue to be drawn from the canal will not come up to the speculation of the English subscribers: but be that as it may the communication will be of unspeakable advantage to the Highlands.

Whatever visions of a bright tomorrow the carefully crafted prospectus had convinced them of, the 'company of the proprietors of the Crinan Canal' numbered 287 on 8 May 1793, when their Act of Parliament received the Royal Assent, allowing the project to proceed. That impressive number of 'proprietors' included several companies, such as Messrs Archibald and Duncan Campbell of Greenock and the Easdale Slate Company. There were 14 women listed – interesting, when Mary Wollstonecraft's *A Vindication of the Rights of Woman* had just been published in 1792 and the idea of female rights conceived by the French Revolution was in general greeted in Britain with the same terror that the Revolution itself engendered. There were, not surprisingly given the location of the Crinan Canal, more Campbells on the list than you could shake a stick at. These went from the highest rank – His Grace, John, Duke of Argyll, along with Rt Hon Lord Frederick Campbell, Lord John Campbell and George, Marquis of Lorne – through a raft of cadet families to the more lowly members of the clan. John, Earl of Breadalbane, co-headed the list with the Duke of Argyll. Birmingham industrialists were on it. John Rennie was on it. And William Pulteney MP, who could be described as Thomas Telford's mentor, was one of nine Members of Parliament who bought shares. The City of Glasgow, Glasgow Chamber of Commerce, landowners in the area of the canal such as Neill Malcolm of Duntrune, Robert McLachlan of Dunadd and Lachlan MacTavish of Dunardry, and John MacNeill of Gigha, benefactor of Ardrishaig and Lochgilphead, were also among the Scots subscribers. Humphrey Graham, who would head up the company from Inveraray, was yet another who bought into the project.

Even so, there was a remarkable number of English shareholders, including ten reverend gentlemen and what seems to be the entire hierarchy of the Wedgwood organisation – Josiah, John, Josiah Junior and Thomas. From the range of the subscribers and their addresses throughout the British Isles, it is clear that the prospectus had done its job. Although some of the links may seem obscure, it is interesting to note that Cathcart, Watt and Wedgwood were tied in that odd late-eighteenth century way that saw men of different classes rubbing along cheek by jowl.

We have seen that Watt and Cathcart had links of locality that brought them together in the earliest days of the planning of the canal. Watt then went off to Birmingham and into the engineering world with his partner Matthew Boulton. The industrialists, philosophers and other major figures in the Midlands founded the Lunar Society, a gentleman's dining club where the issues of the day were discussed. Some of the meetings were held at Boulton's house and regular attenders were Watt and Wedgwood. Watt, with his interest in chemistry, had been involved in a Glasgow pottery before heading south to Birmingham. If we compare the Delftfield Pottery, to which Watt was a technical adviser, and Wedgwood's (which had been established in 1759), we are perhaps envisaging carthorse and Arab stallion. In the 1760s, Queen Charlotte had appointed Wedgwood 'queen's potter'. Delftfield made everyday earthenware. However, Watt and Wedgwood saw only this common bond of similar manufacture, and it was Watt and Boulton who had introduced Wedgwood to Watt's close acquaintance, Lord Cathcart. With the British economy in the doldrums, Boulton, with his knowledge of foreign markets, asked Cathcart to seek out contracts for Wedgwood during his time as ambassador to Catherine II, Empress of Russia, from 1768 to 1772. Perhaps the most profitable order was the 952-piece dinner service the Empress ordered in 1793 for the Chesme Palace.

And all of these people (even if they were more able to stick a pin in the map on St Petersburg's Lake Ladoga than Argyll's Loch Fyne) wanted to buy into the Crinan Canal.

3

The drama begins

In the twenty-first century, if a rail route is to be built or a motorway is planned, the individuals and companies on whose land construction will take place go through a process of negotiation for compensation. There are mechanisms such as compulsory purchase orders. Those who seek to build and those who object or wish to receive more for their house or farm than is being offered all hire their teams of lawyers. And however amicable or acrimonious the process may become, there is a rulebook. Flout the rules and the scandals make headlines. Prison sentences might well ensue. One of our modern rules would involve 'conflict of interest' – an issue that does not seem to have been of any remote concern in the late eighteenth century.

There were, of course, a number of lairds across whose lands the 'Dell' route of the Crinan Canal would pass. They may have wondered about this word 'Dell' – a Lowland corruption of the Gaelic word 'daill', meaning 'meadow'. One was MacTavish of Dunardry, another was Malcolm of Duntroon, or 'of Poltalloch', as the family was alternately styled (there was an old Poltalloch house long before the mid-nineteenth-century mansion of that name was built). These families flit in and out of the canal's story, but at the time of planning and commencement of construction, the spotlight turns on them because of what at this distance seems to be a 'conflict of interest' issue. The MacTavish seat was an ancient one. In the middle of the fourteenth century, Duncan M'Thamais was a Baron of Argyll, and as part of the inner Campbell Clan the MacTavishes held the lands of Dunardry, Dunans, Bardarroch and Barindaff from the Earls (later Dukes) of Argyll. As the earls and dukes dipped in and out of favour during the tempestuous seventeenth century, so Dunardry was confiscated and returned to the MacTavish clan. There was a degree of prosperity in the early to mid-eighteenth century, but times became hard, rents weren't paid and Lachlan MacTavish fell into so much debt he had to put up his lands for sale in 1785. It is hard to tell, given our twenty-first-century perspective, what a come-down it may have been for Lachlan MacTavish to then have to take a job. It was possibly not a 'job' as we know it – perhaps more of a sinecure for which his friends had recommended him. However it was viewed, the facts of the matter were that he went to work at the tax office in James's Court in Edinburgh as an Assistant Surveyor General of Window and House Duty. And whatever his salary may have been, it was not enough to buy back even part of the Dunardry Estate. Colonel John Campbell of Barbreck had been the 1785 buyer, and then in 1792 he put it back on the market. Neill Malcolm of Poltalloch bought Lot 1, comprising the farms of Dunardry, Bardarroch, Barinluaskin (Barnluasgan, according to some spellings), Barindaff (Barrandaimh) and Bellanoch, paying £6,100 for the bundle. This cash was to be paid in two instalments: £2,100 on 11 November 1793, and £4,000 on Whit Sunday, 1797.

This sounds like a reasonable arrangement, and even more

so as Neill Malcolm had done a deal with Lachlan MacTavish: his sole intention in buying the farms was to restore Dunardry, Dunans and Bardarroch to their original owner. MacTavish promised to pay up and so regain his clan seat. Sadly, with his health going downhill and his job at the tax office not yielding enough to meet his promise, MacTavish died in 1796. Neill Malcolm wrote in August 1796 to his lawyer that he had been left with '. . . the whole burthen on my shoulders at a time when money is not easily procured'. In time, Simon McTavish (the different spelling suggests a distant relative), appointed as guardian of Lachlan MacTavish's children, reimbursed Neill Malcolm to the tune of £5,100 from his fortune made as a founder of the Northwest Coalition of Companies in Canada. The period between Malcolm's purchase of the MacTavish farms and MacTavish's death was, of course, when major negotiations for land for the Crinan Canal were enacted.

It is difficult to imagine the lie of the land prior to the construction of the canal – the waterway has given the whole area a distinct boundary. But in the early 1790s there was only the meandering estuary of the River Add broadening out into Loch Crinan at Crinan Ferry. The farms that Neill Malcolm bought were all to the south of the line the canal would take. To the north of the Add was the sprawling moss that James Gow would drain for the Malcolms. In *A treatise on the origin, qualities, and cultivation of moss-earth: with directions for converting it into manure* by William Aiton for the Highland Society of Scotland, published in 1811, the author wrote that 'it must be gratifying to every patriotic mind, to know that the spirit of industry which begins to appear in other parts of Britain, has also found its way into the remote and rugged regions of Argyll'.

With a typical flourish of the day, Aiton added: 'The inhabitants of the district will, I trust, become as famous in agriculture as their ancestors were in arms, when they set the Roman Legions at defiance.'

The distinguished Argyll historian and archaeologist *amateur*, Miss Marion Campbell of Kilberry, has told us that there was a fine trade going on around Crinan in Roman times, when wine from sunny climes was traded for local minerals. Mr Aiton seems to have drawn heavily on legend (or indeed, imagination) to make this claim that the locals saw off the legions. He was on more solid ground with his report of contemporary events, and his flattery of the inhabitants of Argyll was in response to Neill Malcolm's employment of James Gow from 1797 in the main to drain around 600 acres of the Crinan Moss (Mòine Mhòr) and turn them into pasture. Gow, who had gained expertise in such work at Trafford Moss, opened drains, cut trenches, sub-divided the land into sections, planted potatoes in lazy beds and ultimately was able to graze sheep there (Aiton said he would have preferred to see cattle during his visit to Duntroon but was impressed by the progress).

It is clear from the work that Neill Malcolm carried out in the 1790s and early 1800s (Neill Malcolm I would die on 1 April 1802, to be succeeded by Neill Malcolm II) that despite living for much of the year in London, he was determined to make his Argyll estate profitable. He was all in favour of the Crinan Canal (and, of course, had bought some of the £50 shares) but his investment in his estate created the necessity to negotiate the best deal for himself and for the Dunardry farms, whether or not MacTavish was able to take them back into clan ownership. One of the people he employed to help him and MacTavish to do that was John Paterson, the engineer

THE DRAMA BEGINS

appointed by James Watt to oversee the construction of the canal. Paterson was an odd character, as we shall see, and it is an oddity in itself why John Rennie would have employed a man whom he had to send to England to get hands-on experience on the Lancaster Canal before tackling Crinan. In truth, this was a new science and perhaps Paterson was no less experienced than any other Scottish engineer at the time. Be that as it may, Paterson became a frequent visitor at Duntroon in the coming years, dining there and advising on a range of topics, including where to purchase lime for fertiliser in Leith and how to build a house at Bellanoch, producing sketches which he made bold to suggest could best be discussed over dinner at Duntroon. All this while Paterson was in the employ of Rennie and reporting to the canal commissioners in Inveraray. From the archived correspondence, there seems to be no effort to cover this juggling of allegiances. It is tempting to suggest that Mr Malcolm needed Paterson on board and therefore was willing to offer him the occasional dinner; and that Paterson enjoyed hobnobbing with the local laird. It can only be concluded from the relationship that the past was indeed a foreign country and as L.P. Hartley pointed out: 'they do things differently there'. In not a single letter is the phrase 'conflict of interest' evident, however vituperative and accusatory Paterson's correspondence in regard to the canal might become in later years and however frustrated the canal company may have become with him.

Neill Malcolm and Lachlan MacTavish shared in a gentlemanly way a desire to achieve both the restoration to MacTavish of the Dunardry lands (for their different reasons) and the best deal in terms of the canal. Investing in it was one thing, but it was, after all, their lands that would be dug out, their farms through which fishing and coal boats and Baltic traders were expected to sail. What damage would this cause, beyond the lost acreage? What inconveniences would there be? It seemed essential to Neill Malcolm that he and MacTavish be best prepared. And so, another now-famous name seems to have been useful to this pair not only in gauging the value of the Dunardry parcel of farms but in seeking appropriate valuations in order to claim compensation once the canal project went ahead.

On a far grander scale than Neill Malcolm's agricultural developments, the 5th Duke of Argyll was modernising his estates at the end of the seventeenth century. The duke employed George Langlands (today remembered for his work as a cartographer) and his son, Alexander, as agricultural advisors and surveyors from 1771 to 1810 – that crucial period when all the planning and construction (and re-construction) of the Crinan Canal took place. The canal was a pet project of the duke, so Langlands must frequently have been in Mid Argyll and by 1801 he was able to produce a detailed map of the area. In June 1792, a year before the canal was given the parliamentary go-ahead, Neill Malcolm wrote to MacTavish not only about the value of the five farms and their expected rentals but what the situation might be if and when the canal came to fruition. By this time subscribers (including Malcolm himself) had already signed on the dotted line, Watt's and Rennie's surveys had been pored over, and decisions taken about the line of the waterway. Wasn't Langlands the best person to provide him and MacTavish with a bit of insider information? Clearly, asking outright wasn't going to get the answers they wanted, so Malcolm suggested:

> . . . there appears to me a greater necessity that Mr Langlands should go over the ground without knowing

with what intention only to report what rent the land of each farm ought reasonably to yield and by that rental to estimate their value without having at all in view the benefits that might arise from the completion of the canal and perhaps if such an estimate be taken the less we say of our agreement the better for if we suffer the little lack of friends in the country to interfere they will rather mar than forward the business.

This at the time that MacTavish was writing to the Duke of Argyll to say that the prospectus for the canal had been well done, utilising as it did material garnered from 'all the impartial' to promote the advantages of the canal. It does rather seem that MacTavish and Malcolm could not really describe themselves as 'impartial'.

There was also a degree of the pot calling the kettle going on in the area as settlements were slowly but surely made for the land through which the canal would pass. MacNeill of Gigha was another of the landowners to be affected. The Loch Fyne entrance to the canal was to be made at Àird Driseig, 'the promontory of the small bramble'. At the time, there were certainly more brambles (blackberries) to be seen on the promontory than there were houses. What became the village of Ardrishaig had appeared as far back as the 1654 Blaeu map, but when Watt and then Rennie identified a place to create an entrance to the proposed canal, they could count on just one hand the number of dwellings at the Point. MacNeill of Gigha was the proprietor of this land, and owned nearby Oakfield, a house of some distinction (later known as Auchendarroch). As the canal would affect much of this land, he jumped with alacrity on the compensation bandwagon. MacTavish expressed great indignation in a letter written on

30 November 1794 to his friend and relative Coll Lamont of Moneydrain (a property just half a mile from the canal banks). Lamont was away in the army, but he was obviously involved in the compensation claim game, and he may well have experienced *Schadenfreude* when he read MacTavish's letter.

> You would probably hear what a villainous demand for damages Mr McNeill [*sic*] had made – not less at one time than Five & twenty thousand pounds. After a long treaty which retarded the work for more than three months he came down to £3,000, but even that would not be agreed & a Jury was appointed who found him intitled [*sic*] to £1600 only, which after all I consider to be £1000 more than he sh'd [sic] have got.

This from the man who two years previously was in communication with his other neighbour, Mr Malcolm, about hoodwinking George Langlands into unknowingly giving the kind of information that may have allowed them to make their own 'villainous demand' on the Canal Management Committee. These demands and settlements continued as the canal construction proceeded. MacNeill may have received a fraction of his compensation claim, but in the long run he won out because not only did he get more than the valuation put on the land: he owned plenty more in the neighbourhood and was able to develop Ardrishaig and Lochgilphead as the canal entrance developed and the project began to cry out for inns, then houses and commercial buildings. He would have been able to invest his £1,600 in these and would certainly not have been weeping in the dark watches of the night over what the court decided he was 'intitled' to.

THE DRAMA BEGINS

When MacTavish wrote to Coll Lamont of Moneydrain, 400 men had already dug from the point of the brambles well past Moneydrain, despite the three-month hold-up while the MacNeill claim was deliberated over. What is clear, however, is that not only was land being bought up on an ad-hoc basis, but that despite Rennie having apparently decided on the 'Dell' route, this clearly was not set in stone even by the winter of 1794. MacTavish told Lamont: 'It is not yet determined what direction [the canal] is to take from Cairnbaan – whether by Dunardry or Dunadd, but the Directors will determine that sometime next month.'

By the spring of 1795, the 'Dell' plan was back on track, Dunardry was the chosen route from Cairnbaan (and how everyone would rue the day that decision was made!), and Neill Malcolm was being offered £387.5s.7½d in compensation. This was for some 24 acres at an average of around £16 an acre and perhaps Malcolm was hoist by his own petard. Had this been the figure that Langlands, without being told the full reasons for the request for a valuation, placed on the Dunardry property that Malcolm found himself landed with because of MacTavish's misfortune, ill health and subsequent inability to buy back? A period of 30 years' rental was deemed suitable reparation. Humphrey Graham, who was in the employ of the Duke of Argyll, had been a soldier with him and was now appointed as Secretary to the Committee of Management of the Crinan Canal, explained to Neill Malcolm in March 1795 that this was according to Mr Langland's plan for this part of the canal and associated works, stretching across a 148-foot-wide area. If the canal were to take up more or less ground than stipulated, Malcolm would either have to give back some of his compensation or receive more. The £387.5d.7½d was for the ground only.

An arbiter was to be appointed to deal with the loss of trees, houses and stone dykes. Neill Malcolm told the committee that he respected Mr Langlands' 'integrity' and suggested to MacTavish that a gentleman named John MacBrain (already appointed as MacNeill of Gigha's arbiter) be asked to act as for them. Langlands would be the committee's arbiter.

These sums for compensation went, of course, to the landowners. Tenants on these lands were also affected. In early 1795, Captain Duncan MacTavish was far from happy with the claim for damages he faced because of the loss of houses. His lawyer, Neil McGibbon of Inveraray, wrote that the canal would 'sweep away the whole Houses of Dunardry except those of Taynaliskan' and that the complications of his lease, his actual damages and his inconvenience would not be 'regulated by what the Canal Company may pay the proprietor of the land'. There were, in fact, eight houses at Dunardry farm and another at Bardarroch that would be demolished to make way for the course of the canal. People were living out their lives in those houses. They had lazy beds and made their living from their sub-tenancies. The uncertainty of their situation and that of other 'ordinary' people meant they didn't know if a year from then they would have a roof over their heads or a means of surviving. While Lachlan MacTavish was worried in 1795 that if these tenants didn't sow their crops they wouldn't be able to pay their rents (one of the root causes of his own loss of property and face – and the cause of Neill Malcolm to borrow money that spring to keep out of debt because of the Dunardry situation), the anxiety of those most directly affected must surely have been almost unbearable.

It is clear from McGibbon's letter that 'the bottom of Dunardry [would] be sadly cut up by the canal and so will The Bog [the Moss]' and it would be difficult to find stances for the houses that were to come down. MacTavish's motivation may have been less than philanthropic, but his suggestion that the Canal Management Committee allow tenants to reap the 1795 crop before ground was broken for the canal was surely one that would have helped people to survive the following winter. Duncan MacTavish, however, was all for making the tenants who were moved (the plan was to replant them towards the Crinan end of the canal) provide the labour to build their new houses as a cost-cutting exercise. Taking them away from their agricultural work to put roofs over their own heads could only have added to the distress of those whose labours kept all the estates running but who were least likely to be compensated for maximum disruption to their lives.

In theory, those who had bought into the Crinan Canal dream would receive their dividends from the profits. Some had even bigger dreams. In 1793, Neill Malcolm had asked George Langlands to survey for another canal – to link the new Crinan Canal to Loch Awe. It was a good idea – linking the people living on the shores of Loch Awe to this new access to fresh markets. Boats, barges and flat-bottomed boats would offer 'water carriage' of about 45 miles from Lochgilphead. Langlands suggested that from Duntroon via Kilmartin the cost would be £1,255.15s.6½d, while via Kilmichael it would be £15,816, with an 'aqueduct bridge across Kilmartin'. Access to 'the commerce of those parts of the kingdom' would relieve the Loch Awe folk of spending their summers stockpiling fuel for winter, as coal could be imported, while salmon, pearls and local produce could be taken to the markets of the Clyde estuary. The lead mines at Tyndrum would benefit, timber could be transported – what was there not to favour in such a plan? Again, subscriptions would be the way to finance the project. But the increasing problem throughout that decade and into the next was the precarious finances of the country and of individuals as wars and threats of wars began to bite. The Crinan–Awe Canal, following a route that many millennia past had been the slow channel of an Ice Age glacier, was never to leave Langlands' drawing board.

4

The cost of pozzolana and other inconveniences of war

John Rennie was employed at a fee of 200 guineas a year to oversee the building of the Crinan Canal. The contract stipulated that he would attend all the London meetings and then spend a month each year on site. Mr Rennie's star was rising, however, and he had bridges to build, other canals to construct, docks to plan, so many other contracts to fulfil. And so, by 1794 – the year that work began in the September – his salary was cut to 100 guineas because he had persuaded the Canal Committee that he did not need to be on site. Instead, John Paterson was to oversee the project and report to the Canal Committee at its new office in Inveraray. It is easy to see why Paterson would welcome not just a dinner at Duntroon but a bed for the night, because travel from the site to Inveraray, a distance by today's roads of around 27 miles from the Loch Fyne entrance to the canal, could take a whole day. The Inveraray Inn, designed by John Adam and opened under the name of The Great Inn in 1755 as the Duke of Argyll's planned new town sprang into being, would have been somewhere for Samuel Johnson and James Boswell, Robert Burns, and Dorothy

Wordsworth to stay. Paterson may have found himself in less salubrious quarters.

It was he who would for several years be in charge of employing men (as many as 600 labourers are mentioned in some records, many from Ireland, many who had experience of working on canals in England, and, of course, some local men), negotiating with contractors and supervising the work itself. To the layperson, digging out the canal seems in theory to be the simplest part of the job. However, because of the mixed nature of the terrain, this was not in reality the case. One day the men may have been battling with soft peat moss or whinstone, the next blasting their way through granite. Explosives were, in the 1790s, neither sophisticated nor as accessible to the construction industry as the subscribers to the Crinan Canal project may have believed to be the case.

Saltpetre had been of little value in the first half of the seventeenth century, seen mainly as ballast for ships. Various conflicts, including wars with Indian Mughals in the 1660s, put saltpetre on the map as a valuable commodity in making explosives. By the end of the Seven Years War (1756–63), the first conflict fought across a global arena, the Treaty of Paris put control of Bengal saltpetre in British hands. As saltpetre was the main ingredient of gunpowder and Bengal was its main source, this gave Britain a hugely important advantage. However, although the price was right in peacetime for construction work such as blasting through rock for canal building, its use in weaponry meant that in wartime not only did the price shoot through the roof but it was also rationed in favour of the military forces. And, of course, the year that parliament gave permission for the Crinan Canal project to proceed was the year that hostilities between France and Britain broke out as part of the French Revolutionary Wars, which from 1799 to 1815 turned into the Napoleonic Wars. As well as its price going up, gunpowder was in ever-shorter supply, as the various French blockades bit into Britain's imports. This wasn't good news in terms of the canal funding. This was not a good time (or indeed a good place) to be building a canal on a limited budget.

The letters from canal company secretary Colonel Graham, writing from the Crinan Canal office in Inveraray to landowners such as Neill Malcolm of Poltalloch and MacNeill of Gigha, pointing out the inconveniences their failure to agree on compensation was causing was just a part of the story. A few weeks' – or even months' – delay in pushing through to Moneydrain or Dunardry was not, however, caused solely by such negotiations. The French had a lot to answer for. The trouble at the Dunardry section, which was to cause such grief for so many workers, surveyors and engineers (not to mention the Canal Committee and the subscribers) over the coming years, could be blamed on Napoleon Bonaparte's belligerence – and John Paterson's stubborn refusal to accept he was faced with a problem caused by external forces. That problem was the lack of appropriate materials to do the job.

Pozzolana is the Italian name for a very special ingredient of waterproof cement. The Romans used pozzolana in their underground sewers and their overland aqueducts. It comes from Pozzuoli, near Naples. It is present in volcanic ash, reacts with calcium hydroxide and sets in water to create a cement that allows no water to penetrate. It can set overnight and then lasts for – well, at least 2,000 years, if the evidence of the Roman aqueducts is anything to go by. It would have been ideal for constructing underwater sections of the canal.

Unfortunately, the French placed too many difficulties in the way of transporting pozzolana between southern Italy and Mid Argyll. This, of course, meant that a much less sophisticated type of cement (and cement was, like explosives, still in its infancy) had to be used in constructing the locks at Dunardry. Result: leaks and more leaks.

In a report on the progress of the canal made by John Rennie on 6 September 1796, he notes that the stocks of pozzolana were 'diminished and from the situation of affairs in Italy, there is little hope of getting fresh supplies'. What was left — apparently there was a paltry quantity of the stuff in a warehouse on the Clyde — was to be reserved for the sea lock. Rennie also mentions that in the area of Oakfield 'the lower bank sank 9 feet' and more earth had to be added for a solid foundation. Although the softness of the ground there was the 'only difficulty experienced', as the work progressed west, 'the inequality of the strata' was such that he couldn't tell from one place to the next what the quality would be. 'Rock,' he said, was found 'in situations where none could have been expected', adding that the 'rise in the price of gunpowder has raised the price of rock from 16 to 20s[hillings] per cubic yard'.

Rennie encountered an accumulation of such difficulties. The sea lock at Portree — the old name for Crinan — was causing engineering difficulties; there was a 'deficient supply of oak' from Messrs Muirhead & Co., which meant the carpenter was 'not able to get so forward as he otherwise would have done'; other contractors such as Burns, Muir and Paterson were 'dilatory in the extreme', with work undertaken 'not nearly finished'; law suits over unfinished work were threatened; emergency measures, including 'a buttress of rough stones against the south west of the sea lock to defend it until the pier can be built' [at Ardrishaig]; and Cairncross and Cairns, the contractors at the Crinan end of the canal responsible for rock cutting, had 'likewise been deficient in their exersions [*sic*]'.

Some progress was certainly being made and Rennie always put a positive spin at the start of his reports, whatever bad news the remainder of them contained. Despite the worst storms 'ever remembered', there had been no 'material misfortune or accident'. The sea lock at Ardrishaig was nearly completed and Rennie had 'great hopes we shall be equally successful with the sea lock at Portree which is the principal difficulty in point of engineering we have encountered'. But he had to confess that the foundations of the sea lock at Crinan were in reality going to be tricky, and both boulders and '4 or 5 thousand feet of Scotch fir' were going to have to be purchased to carry out the job properly. Slate from Italy, like the pozzolana, would have done the job, but would not be possible to import because of the international situation. Rennie admitted, 'It is impossible for me under the circumstances . . . to make any accurate estimates of the expense we may pay to finish the works.' Then, with his customary optimism, penned for the directors '. . . but I have my reason to believe it will be considerably under the sum subscribed'.

This, with hindsight, is an obvious spin on the realities. Such an accrual of problems signposted potential disaster, not completion on time and under budget. But then, by March 1797, Rennie was able to tell the Committee of Management that 'the canal may be used in the interim for the carriage of materials, and indeed for the trade itself without waiting for the pier'. This progress must have seemed like a mixed blessing for the Duke of Argyll and his cousin, Breadalbane. The pair had led the campaign to build a canal; now it was almost a reality and perhaps even on the verge of bringing in the promised rewards to them and to their army of subscribers. And yet even as Rennie reported that vessels could now use the waterway, the threat of the wrong vessels, the vessels of invaders using that same canal, was very real and could only have taken the edge off what in better times would have only been cause for celebration.

For a year, the duke had been charged with setting up a very different kind of army — a real one, in the shape of both a militia and a fencible infantry, because of the 'present situation of the country'. The Act to Raise and Embody a Militia Force in Scotland was finally passed on 19 July 1797. Men were conscripted to the militia and the government provided uniforms, weapons and training. The fencible troops were volunteers, but they were paid as regular soldiers. The militia and the fencible infantry, however, were required to serve both at home and abroad. The 1797 Act was intended to create a locally based defence for the whole country and Lords Lieutenant had been appointed in each county since an invasion scare in 1793. These Lords Lieutenant were responsible for both defence and policing, although there would be no formal police force until 1800, when the City of Glasgow became the first in Britain to establish a constabulary. A number of Scottish cities quickly followed suit, but Sir Robert Peel's Act, creating his famous 'Peelers' (a metropolitan force), was not passed until 1829.

In the 1790s, law and order seems still to have been under the rather lax jurisdiction of the Board of Police in Scotland, which had been established in 1714 (Lord Cathcart, that old acquaintance of James Watt's family and one of those who encouraged the building of the canal, had been a president of

THE COST OF POZZOLANA 53

the board before his death in 1776) and was seen as a sinecure for those appointed to it.

At this time of threat of invasion, therefore, it was landowners such as the Duke of Argyll who were responsible for the Fencibles. The duke's eldest son, the Marquis of Lorne, was appointed Lord Lieutenant of Argyllshire. The county had its own Militia Act and, as this was just 50 years after Culloden, the government must have experienced some anxiety over arming and training Highlanders. The Scotland-wide Act required that 6,000 men aged between 18 and 25 be raised for the duration of the war. Men who were married, had two children and assets of £50 were exempt. There were also exemptions for teachers, clergy, apprentices and sailors, but not fishermen, which became a bone of contention in Argyll, where most men spent at least part of the year at sea (and a canal was being constructed to make it easier for them to do so). Little wonder, then, that not everyone was happy to jump to it and join the militia. Indeed, in 1797 there was rioting because the call-up was seen as an infringement of liberty and a discriminatory tax on working men and Gaelic speakers. Gaelic had, of course, been proscribed after Culloden and there was no thought of 'inclusion' when the Act was written, leaving most of the population in Argyll and the Isles ignorant of its intentions.

Throughout the country men suspected that these local militias were just an underhand way of luring men into the regular army, which would mean they could be sent to fight abroad against the French. This suspicion had its basis in fact: the Argyllshire Militia would indeed be sent to fight in Gibraltar and then Ireland in 1798. Reassurances had to be made to avoid trouble. In September 1797, the Mid Argyll Court of Lieutenancy recorded: 'The Meeting having understood that in many parts of Scotland ill-disposed persons had been at pains to mislead the lower orders of the people by a misconstruction of the Act of Parliament . . .', suggesting that there would be trouble if the 'lower orders' weren't enlightened. The outcome was that the Act had to be explained fully in Gaelic and notices had to be displayed on church doors, explaining the intricacies of the conscription procedures, the penalties incurred for failing to serve, who was exempt from serving and the prohibition against militiamen being forcibly enlisted in the regular army. This is an interesting turnaround from the harsh proscription of half a century previously: was it about winning hearts and minds, or simply a necessity to bulk up military forces for a government at war?

It can be seen from the list of exemptions that those with a bit of money and a certain type of job were off the hook. The poorest people had no get-out clause and the small allowance did not compensate families who lost the man of the house to the militia.

The Volunteer Corps of Argyllshire had raised 244 men in 1796, but on 27 February, Colonel Graham (who was also the secretary to the Canal Management Committee) wrote to the Duke of Argyll that some volunteers were remiss in turning up for training and their clothing was now almost worn out. He asked the duke if he could get quotes for new clothing, 'as there are hopes of them appearing in them on His Majesty's birthday'. The Duke of Argyll had in 1794 been asked by George III to raise a kilted regiment. Because of ill health, he delegated the task of raising that regiment, the Argyllshire Highlanders, to Duncan Campbell of Lochnell. Now he was in the thick of it, organising the eighteenth-century equivalent of the Second World War's Home

Guard. Known as a military man, it is revealing to see that when Colonel Graham writes to him about the volunteers' kit, there is as much attention to fashion detail as could be found in *The Lady's Magazine*, a favourite publication of the decade.

'A standing collar would be better than the present,' Colonel Graham suggested to the duke. He added that the coat ought to have a half-facing of scarlet, '. . . such as I have attempted to sketch below, with perhaps a lace hole in the collar and white lining – and as the volunteers here have got black half gaiters and the rest may easily get them, it has occurred that instead of the Duck trousers they might get white cloth breeches'.

How practical was this suggestion? Evidently the clothing allowance for 1795 and 1796 had accrued and some county funding was also to be used for these new uniforms. Samples were to be made up in London. Graham's sketch shows a short blue coat 'turned up with red', a white cloth waistcoat, Duck trousers, white worsted stockings and a helmet. Colonel Graham wondered whether the men should be issued with shoes or be given the money 'to fit themselves, as they were very ill served in 1794'. We know today the importance of kit fit for purpose being issued to troops, but this seems to place undue emphasis on appearance (perhaps with a view to looking good for the king's birthday on 4 June?).

By the next year, Neill Malcolm, now one of the Deputy Lieutenants for the 'Shire of Argyle', had concerns of a different and much more practical kind.

On 2 July 1797, he wrote from Poltalloch to the Duke:

I observe by the second article my attention is particularly requested to the parish of Craignish. Perhaps your Grace does not know that the greatest part of my Estate lyes [sic] round and near to the Bay of Creenan [sic] in the Parish of Kilmartin ... A situation fully as much exposed to the depredation of an enemy as any part of the Shire, and in my humble opinion requiring a Force to be stationed there to repele [sic] any attempts that may be made to effect a landing in so safe and convenient a Harbour.

With this view and a promise made to my Tenants when they so early and cheerfully enrolled themselves that in case of Emergency, I and my Son would take the field at their head, I have resisted the solicitation of some neighbours to let my tenants join their volunteer company, at the same time as I can form a complete company of my own tenants (two if necessary) on both sides of the River Add to meet near the Bay of Creenan, it is but doeing My Son and them justice to declare your Grace their lead ... to come forward whenever Government should require and Your Grace see fit to Form additional Volunteer Companys [sic] for the defence of the country.

The response from the duke on 4 August 1797 was perhaps a little pointed, with a subtext inferring that, because Mr Malcolm seems to spend much of his time at his property in London, he isn't the man for the job (the duke himself was hardly in residence at Inveraray on a permanent basis).

He replied:

When I came to arrange the stations of the twenty companies which the Government thought proper to accept of, instead of the eight battalions that were offered, I did not overlook the Harbour of Crinan.

I recommended to the command of the Company in

that neighbourhood Mr Campbell of Kilmartine[sic], a gentleman in my point of view insusceptionable [sic] and particularly so from his constant residence in the country, which I considered to be very essential. I did not conceive that either you or your son would think of taking the command of a company of volunteers in Argyllshire unless the situation of the kingdom should call for a more general arrangement. It is not however to that single company that the Harbour of Crinan is to look for protection. There is another at Lochgilphead and a third betwixt Lochgair and Kilmichael, situations from whence I presume the whole could assemble at any point about Crinan in case of need in three or four hours.

If however you should think it necessary, you may be supplied with a certain quantity of arms if your People should incline to learn to use them without pay, as others do.

The fact that Mr Malcolm's lands stretched along the shores of Loch Crinan, the canal ran through them and the location of his 'People' put them just minutes from any scene of action (rather than three or four hours away on the shores of Loch Fyne) suggests that the Duke was playing a game of one-upmanship here.

By December of that year, the Militia Act was revised to raise more men if and when necessary. Wars are far-reaching, and while the burden on those who have least is always the greatest, the costs are always spread across the whole of society and for generations to come. As far as the Crinan Canal is concerned, the effects of the Napoleonic Wars stretch across more than two centuries. We know that for want of a nail, the shoe, horse, rider, message, battle and kingdom were lost. For want of affordable gunpowder, what lay beneath the waterline of the Crinan Canal remained jagged with unmoveable rocks. For want of pozzolana, leaking locks threatened the very existence of the canal from its earliest days. Napoleon may not have invaded Britain through the Crinan Canal, but he certainly affected its efficiency.

5

The want of a nail

Work began on the canal in September 1794. Despite the want of pozzolana and gunpowder, signed contracts to allow hundreds of men to dig a massive trench across landowners' property meant progress was surprisingly rapid. The war was a backdrop that created a range of problems, but the more everyday difficulties presented by Argyll's climate and landscape caused greater glitches in the canal's development. There were the storms of the winter of 1795-96. The 'sudden floods' in the Waters of Gilp and Dunardry that Rennie reported arose 'from the sudden deluges of rain which frequently fall on the hills south of the summit level, which the locks in their present state are unable to contain for any considerable time'. During 1796 he also reported that the sea lock at Portree was now the major engineering (and fiscal) challenge because the foundation was 'part rock and the other a sandy clay of the worst sort which makes it difficult to form an artificial foundation able to sustain the weight of such a superstructure'. He warned that 'should one part yield more than another a fracture in the masonry must be the infallible consequence and perhaps the destruction of the lock itself'. In another part of the construction work, the softness of the sand on which the banking of Bellanoch Bay was laid had, according to Rennie's September 1797 report, 'sunk full as much as that at the entrance of the moss of Oakfield and the ground on the outside has risen proportionately'. Rennie advised another survey, and warned that if material could not be used to hold the mud and create a safe enough channel, 'the canal must be carried round the Head of the bay, which will make a very awkward turn'.

Today's engineering experts suggest that Rennie created some of the problems that beleaguered the canal from its outset to the present day. One of his persistent design faults, seen on this canal and others he built, was the very short summit that caused major water-supply problems. The Crinan Canal summit was just three-quarters of a mile long. There is a flight of four big locks at one side and five locks at the other. Depth is another criticism made of Rennie's work by modern engineers — but let's not forget that the vessels for which Rennie's canals were designed were much smaller than those introduced once steam power was adapted to waterborne vessels. The *Comet*, the first steam-powered vessel, was not launched until 1812.

Indeed, Rennie updated his plans, enlarging the canal dimensions at some points. Out at the Crinan sea lock, for example, the channel was, in 1797, 27 feet wide with 16 feet of water, instead of the planned 24 feet wide and 12 feet of water. Rennie's complaint was the difficulties in getting vessels big enough to carry the stone required to line the locks rather than that the canal was too small for the vessels.

This was the year that he began work on the Kennet and Avon Canal in the south of England. It was an important project, with an aqueduct on a stretch in the Wiltshire countryside. He knew that the Kennet and Avon Canal Company had '200 tons of pozzolana to dispose of', while the Crinan Canal management had only 60 tons at its disposal. He suggested in his September report that the Crinan company try to negotiate with the English canal people to buy 100 tons for £4 to £5 a ton, 'unless it can be found elsewhere for less'. The trouble was, the pozzolana might as well have still been in Rome as in Hungerford because £400 to £500 was stretching the budget of the Crinan Canal Company just too far. Accounts submitted the previous December revealed massive bills – £1,062.16s.6½d for a steam engine, £2,836.13s.6¾d for timber (not to mention a further £216.13s.5¼d for oak purchased at Drumlanrig in Dumfriesshire), and £5,320.4s paid to the contractors Andrew Brocket. The Act of Parliament itself, which involved engraving of plans and printing of bills, had cost £726.11s.10d, and officers' salaries amounted to £2,473.12s.1d. All in all, £108,456.3s.2½d had drained from the canal company's coffers, and the canal stock as of 31 December 1796 stood at £107,900.

What a pity Dickens' Mr Micawber was half a century away, with his salutary advice to David Copperfield: 'Annual income twenty pounds, annual expenditure nineteen, nineteen and six, result happiness. Annual income twenty pounds, annual expenditure twenty pounds ought and six, result misery.' The Crinan Canal Company was already struggling to keep its head above the ten feet of water in the canal when Rennie suggested buying in the pozzolana from the south of England. He had predicted in his March 1797 report that 'should money come regularly in, there is little doubt of the Canal being finished in the course of the next year'. But by the September he had written to the governor of the canal directors to say, 'I am still under the disagreeable necessity of saying that some of the contractors have not proceeded with that diligence and expedition which the interest of the undertaking requires.'

He sacked the company of Muir, Paterson and Burns because the pier at Ardrishaig was 'as yet untouched'. Mr Brocket, the builder, was also labelled as 'dilatory', and Rennie described the delay in masonry work at Ardrishaig locks as 'unpardonable'. On the plus side (and he needed some positives to report), the work at Oakfield was nearly finished and Rennie said that it had 'turned out better than any on the canal, very little rock having been found in it'. It was William Gardner who had been responsible for this piece of the project. He was contracted to do the summit work and, at the end of September 1797, still had work on the lock and cutting to complete between Dunamuck Mill and Cairnbaan. By 1 November 1798, a year and eight months after Rennie's prediction of completion by the end of 1798, funds were short and bills went unpaid. It was time to heed the Micawber principle. The sea lock at 'Portree' was finished, except for the hanging of the lock gates, which would be done in December 1798, if the weather held out. The second lock was just two months away from being completed. With his usual public face of confidence, Rennie therefore suggested that a cofferdam (a temporary enclosure constructed within the canal channel that could be drained to make a dry work environment where finishing work could take place) should be built 'and the steam engine disposed of'.

This engine was, he said, 'one of the completest machines of its kind in Scotland, and little if anything worse for the use'. An offer had been made for it of £425 – Rennie insisted that 'nothing less than £500 should be taken'. It had, of course, cost more than twice that. It is worth remembering that steam engines such as this (designed and produced by Rennie's friend Watt in Birmingham) were also in their infancy, but selling like hot cakes because of their efficiency in pumping water from mines and canal works. Rennie was right that it was a seller's market. However, against the grand scale of the mounting debts, trying to sell off a capital asset for £500 seems a futile gesture – but at least Rennie was attempting to stem the tide of outgoing cash.

The end of 1798 would not see completion of the project, but Rennie didn't think he was too far out in his estimates. It would, he wrote, take around four months, 'God willing', for work to be completed by Macarthur & Co. on the stretch between the Point of Crinan and the March of Taynloan (*sic*). The section between Cairnbaan and Ardrishaig had had eight feet of water in it for six months and appeared to be watertight in all but a few places. Rennie said that this section had been used 'to convey vessels loaded with materials from Greenock, Arran [the best quality freestone] and other places for the locks now building in the Vale of Dunamuck'. He was keeping all the balls in the air, but the company was threatening to do a deal with the contractors and pull the plug on the project. Rennie needed to convince the directors to hold their nerve. He added in his 1 November 1798 report:

> However deficient therefore the funds may prove for the letting of new contracts, I trust sufficient money will be reserved for the finishing of these [bottom cleaning, bank raising, etc.] as I am sure were a settlement to be made with the contractors in their present state it would be greatly against the company.

It is clear that although he was not spending the originally contracted time at the canal, Rennie was certainly trying to ensure that the canal was completed, and completed well. However distant this was from the work he was involved with in England — or even Leith — it was still being done in his name and he had a reputation to maintain. A shoddy little canal in the remote West Highlands of Scotland would present as big a black mark against his name as a problematic bridge construction in Leith or London. He wisely carried out yet another survey, this time on the locks that were completed or in the process of being completed.

'I find the floods may be more completely managed than at first I was sure of,' he told the Committee of Management in correspondence received on 4 January 1799. 'In heavy rains the floods are beyond imagination as when compared with their low state in an ordinary season.'

But he had no intention of letting the management off the hook for its role in the faltering progress. Rennie didn't spare the Committee of Management's feelings in this early 1799 communication. He did, however, with the politesse of the late eighteenth century, preface his remarks with the phrase, 'who have been constantly attentive to the interest of the concern'. Then he delivered the bullet, telling them they had 'never been able to act in the effective manner I expect they could have done had they been sure of paying the debt they contracted'. He added:

> Many material pieces of work have been left behind which should have been done and all my prognostications of the time of finishing the work disappointed. Unless more effective means of raising money are pursued, which should be done before February, it is in vain my attempting to fix any time for the completion of the work or indeed its cost for every day the sea lock at Ardrishaig

remains unprotected, the more gravel and silt will get into it.

It was time for a bit of market research to stiffen the sinews of the canal management and reassure the subscribers. A similar exercise had, of course, been carried out in order to convince those subscribers (and the politicians who passed the Crinan Canal Act), but careful reading of MacTavish's comments to the Duke of Argyll about the time constraints on the production of that first prospectus suggest that the modern concept of market research and the process carried out in the early 1790s may not have much in common. Now in March 1799 there was some quite detailed projection for the future success of the canal.

The Fishing Trade in Grangemouth was expected, once the canal was finished, to send some 60 vessels 'averaging 60 tons burthen each' through the canal 'both going and returning from the fishing'. Greenock and Port Glasgow expected 122 vessels, totalling 7,806 tons, to use the canal. Ayr had already sent 468 tons through in the year to 5 January 1798, suggesting that Rennie and his team had got something right. Campbeltown craft in 1798 had totalled 50, with a 'burthen of 2,113 tons'. The authorities in Campbeltown, which had lost 400 guineas 'from having been harbour bound in Campbeltown' in the previous two years, thought the canal dues were well worth it. Stranraer estimated 14 vessels would use the canal. Rothesay and Bute presented an interesting case study. The island exported herring to Ireland and imported grain from Ireland. It was reported that the 'greater part of the vessels belonging to the port of Rothesay during the time they are disengaged from the fishing are employed in this trade of exporting their herrings to Ireland and bringing back grain, meal and other articles in return'. The estimate of their trade was 8,371 barrels. Eight barrels weighed a ton, so they were looking at taking 10,464 tons through the canal. The 1799 report said that their own vessels and those from a number of other Clyde ports that traded with Ireland 'will take the canal'. To the landlubber, this may not seem like a particularly direct route, but the report says:

> It is a well known fact that vessels bound for these ports from Clyde are frequently driven far to the northward after they have doubled the Mull of Kintyre, by the strong currents and south west winds, which may be called the trade winds of the western coasts, and also when returning with grain etc., they are forced to take shelter so far to the northwards as Mull, Tyree [sic], Canna, etc. But when the canal is opened, the greater part of the inconveniences, expence [sic] and damage, now experienced in continuing with the Mull of Kintyre will be avoided.

The reasoning of the Rothesay experts was that 'the wages and victualing alone of the crews for their time lost in doubling the Mull would pay the canal dues'. Another factor cited in favour of the canal was a possible lowering of insurance premiums. Insurance of a kind has operated since Babylonian times, but, in its modern sense, marine insurance began in the 1680s, with the opening of Lloyd's Coffee House in London. Informal meetings there of all involved with maritime matters led to the formalised Lloyd's of London and other insurance companies specialising in covering marine businesses (the Society of Lloyd's in the Royal Exchange in Cornhill was opened in 1774). The expectation in 1799 was that 'the premium of insurance on herrings exported will probably be lowered one and a half per cent in consequence of the opening of the canal'.

The market research stretched to those trading out of North America and the Baltic. The Newfoundland, Halifax and Canadian Traders expected that a 'very large proportion' of their 2000-3000-ton trade would 'take the canal, especially in the Fall and Winter seasons'. Anything that would guarantee their vessels were not storm-bound in Lamlash, Arran, by southerly winds or being driven north to Mull, Canna, Skye and Tiree could only be regarded in a favourable light. Baltic traders reported that their insurance premiums had risen and their trade had dropped because of the risks involved. The opening of the Crinan Canal would 'enable the most remote corners to participate'. And even though traders to the Baltic obviously required larger vessels than the herring boats, it was suggested that 'vessels employed in the trade to Norway, Sweden, Hamburg, Archangel, Minsk, etc., are generally of such dimensions that three-quarters of them might pass through the canal'.

Minsk? This was the age of canals, and the Dnieper–Bug Canal, known then as the Royal Canal, constructed between 1775 and 1784, was an important part of a transportation artery linking the Baltic and Black Seas. This meant that the Baltic traders could reach the then-Polish inland city of Minsk. The Royal Canal was 122 miles long – a little more impressive than the Crinan Canal, but both were planned to develop wider markets.

There were convoys sailing to the Baltic in the 1790s. Vessels from Saltcoats, Irvine, Ayr, Stranraer, Dumfries, Whitehaven, Workington, Maryport, Ulverston, Lancaster, Liverpool, Belfast, Dublin, Cork and other Irish ports had cargoes that included slates, kelp, lime and limestone, shell and sand, timber, bark and charcoal. The Western Isles and West Highland ports exported 7,000 tons of kelp annually. Sometimes whole convoys were lost. Sometimes it was a case of running to Lamlash and Lochranza for shelter. It is easy to see why the concept of the Crinan Canal appealed so much to these traders. No one wants to pay high insurance premiums. No one wants to pay extra wages because of wasted working days. No one wants to lose valuable cargoes – or lives. The canal seemed to offer an answer to all these problems.

At a more local level, the proposed removal of duty from coals had been implemented, which meant that an increase in sales of coal to the Western Isles was doubly viable with the new shortcut. Tonnage was expected to double. The Act of Parliament had stipulated the tolls and duties that could be levied on vessels going through the canal. Essentials such as coals and salt, lime, limestone, shell and sand, and manure for the land could not be charged at more than two pence sterling per ton per mile. Open boats 'not exceeding seven tons burthen' could not be charged more than 14 pence sterling for each boat per mile. All other vessels and goods could be charged at not more than three pence sterling per ton per mile. The tolls for light boats and other vessels without loading or in ballast only would be one penny per ton of her burden per mile. An estimate of tolls that could be expected from the trade promised by fishing boats from all over Scotland was £8,948.8s.

The report of 1799 said:

> It may be satisfactory to the friends of this undertaking to find that the more minutely the sources of revenue are investigated the more productive they promise to turn out – and the consideration cannot fail of exciting

in all concerned the strongest desire to see this great and beneficial work speedily completed. The Reporters will therefore proceed to show the sum of money that would be required for that purpose by the following estimate.

The figure to complete the canal was £25,423.16s.5½d. An admirably precise sum that included completion of the summit, the stretches from the summit to Baddenoch, March of Baddenoch to Points of Crinan (work had been suspended for eight months but was estimated as being just five months from completion), the embankment at Bellanoch Bay, and the Points of Crinan to the termination of the canal (where the basin would already hold 30 vessels).

Was all this a case of counting chickens before they were hatched? Colonel Graham and John Paterson admitted in March 1799, 'This undertaking has certainly required more money than was first expected, owing in a great measure to the large and in many parts unexpected quantities of rock which have been found in the track thereof – in many places rock has been discovered within a few inches of a mossy surface where none could be expected.' This had meant that realistic calculations of cost and time had not been feasible during surveys. The pair added, 'It is supposed that in no canal executed of its length has so much whinstone rock been blown out.'

Comparisons were made with a canal in France's Languedoc, where 30,000 cubic feet of rock had been excavated in the course of 'about 176 English miles'. This, the reporters hazarded, 'will be considered as nothing when it is known that three hundred and fourteen thousand eight hundred and twenty two cubic yards of whinstone rock has already been turned out of the Crinan Canal, which is about 280 times the quantity of the Languedoc Canal and one twelfth the length'. To blast the 8,500,194 cubic feet of whinstone rock had taken 31,600 pounds of gunpowder (which cost the contractors £2,100); it had cost £1,532.10s.2d for the iron tools (and their sharpening) used in that part of the work, and removal of the rock was costly. In the early 1960s, the rock hewn from within Ben Cruachan, Argyll's highest mountain, in the process of constructing the hydroelectricity project there, was used to create new roads and other land reclamation projects. What a pity engineering had not reached such practical levels 150 years previously. The cost of disposing of the rock seems to have been inordinately disproportionate to the cost of the canal itself.

When Graham and Paterson signed off this report on 26 March 1799, their main message was: 'Give us the money and the canal will be open in 18 months'. But there was no cash in the kitty, and not only did the subscribers have to raise more money, the management had to go cap in hand to the government.

With £10,000 more raised by the company, a government mortgage of £25,000 secured against the projections of tolls and dues suggested by the market research, and the loan of some soldiers to add to the labour force, the canal did indeed open in 1801. After the terrible 1796 setback, when hundreds of yards of canal bank subsided, and the numerous other hold-ups experienced because of technical or monetary difficulties, it was little short of miraculous there was an opening. Indeed fingers and toes must have been crossed because there was nothing technically sound about such a move.

Paterson and Graham reported on 10 April 1801 (a copy was sent to London on 24 April) that the Ardrishaig to Cairnbaan section was finished except the bank in the

Moss of Oakfield, which was expected to be complete by mid-May. Towpath work was still to be carried out, but the report recorded that this would 'not retard navigation'. The section from Cairnbaan to the south end of the summit basins was complete, but banking, the levelling of the towpaths and the public road were still to be completed. Lock work was estimated to take another two weeks. The trunk of the canal on the summit level was finished except for a 'few hundred yards of gravel at each end which could not be excavated until the lock gates in the Vale of Dunamuck were hung'. This was estimated as a three-week job. The banking at the south end of the summit was to be carried out, as was some 4,000–5,000 yards of earth banking between Locks 9 and 13. From Lock 13 to the Points of Crinan, bank cutting was finished except at Bellanoch Bay. Earth was to be brought from Bardarroch on boats. Parts of the Crinan to Portree section were optimistically described as 'almost done', and what was still to be completed could be done so 'in a month with 20 men'. The lock gates were to be hung at Portree and this was to be completed by the end of May. Delays due to bad weather were reported between February and April, but the 'scarcity of money was also felt' and if the cash had been available, it was believed the work could have been completed a month earlier despite the weather.

This 'it's finished except for . . .' report is not enhanced by the comments that reveal the staggering extent of those 'except fors'.

It was foreseen, for example, that without regulation of the water flowing into the summit during wet weather, 'great damage may be occasioned'. It was recommended that the management committee appoint 'two proper persons for lock keepers'. One was to reside in the Vale of Dunamuck and the other at Dunardry. These men were to be of 'known integrity and attention' and they had to know the 'nature of their duty'. A mason or carpenter were suggested as suitable candidates, and their wages were to be 'higher than is generally paid to lock keepers yet it may turn out in the end money well disposed of'. Once the problem of the excess of water in the canal was fixed, 'less well paid lock keepers' could be employed. There was also a need of an 'attentive decent man' at Portree, but the problem there was 'not half the damage' as at the summit.

While lock keepers were being employed because of their skills in tackling possible disasters, more regular needs were also being planned for – 'horses in readiness to draft the vessels along the navigation'. The report reckoned that two horses would be required at each end of the canal because some vessels would need two horses, others just one. There would, of course, be a charge for this work: 'one shilling a mile or nine shillings for each vessel should be a fair price'.

Despite quite major work such as drawbridges over the lock at Dunardry, the ford of the River Add, and the lands of Kilmahumaig, it seems in retrospect that the engineers and the management committee simply sleepwalked their way to the canal being deemed 'open'.

6

The disasters that had been waiting to happen

Teething troubles can always be expected during a new project's early months of operation, but a lengthy stay in the dental hospital should not be on the cards. For the next decade, however, the Crinan Canal was a suitable case for treatment and a range of orthodontists were never far from our heroine's side. Her nine-mile-wide smile revealed some shocking irregularities from the moment she officially opened in 1801. By May 1802, cosmetic work such as fencing was excusable, but surely leaks and sinking banks should have been dealt with before the 'opening'. There was always a 'good news/bad news' element to John Paterson's reports. The good news: at Oakfield the bank 'looks well'. The bad news: 'excepting 100 yards still sinking'.

There were some problems, however, that Paterson could not sugar-coat and increasingly over the next few years he sought instead to pass the buck and blame anyone but the man charged with sorting them: himself. There were leaks from Dunardry to Bellanoch Bay (the old pozzolana problem, no doubt) and a 'considerable quantity of water' had been lost as a result. There had been repairs carried out, but they had not solved the difficulty. There was also ongoing work on the banking at Bellanoch Bay, which had 'given much trouble and occasioned a very considerable extra expense, owing entirely to the softness of the materials it stands upon'. Paterson said that when he left Crinan in February 1801 it had been estimated that 8,000 yards of moss would finish the bank. That should have done the trick and raised the bank high enough to accommodate 12 feet of water. But it had sunk.

In the intervening year, with the canal open for business, a staggering 22,000 yards of moss were laid and still Paterson had to admit that 'there cannot with safety be more than 9ft or 9½ft of water raised on it'. Not to mention the £400 that had been spent on this sticking plaster solution. Paterson made it clear that Mr Rennie had ordered this work to be done in August 1801. Now, in May 1802, it was clearly going to take another 10,000 yards of moss to raise Bellanoch bank to a 'proper height and breadth'. There were also leaks in a three-quarter-mile stretch from Crinan Ferry to Portree, which Paterson described as the 'most difficult part' because the rocks were 60 feet high on the upper side of the canal. One of the contractors reported that repairs here had not succeeded as expected. Another £300 was needed to fix the summit, a repair without which the lock gates would be ruined. And then there were houses to be built for the lock keepers and a dry dock constructed at Portree.

As if this haemorrhaging of funds were not disastrous enough, there were landowners still complaining about lack of compensation and MacNeill of Gigha was circulating pamphlets complaining about the extra land he claimed had been taken for the canal. This is the man who had put in an initial claim for £25,000 and had been knocked back to a sensible sum. Once an opportunist, always an opportunist, but the pips were already squeaking in the Crinan lemon and he would not make another penny from the management committee. MacNeil was not the only 'chancer', in Paterson's eyes – he had tried to beat down a contractor who wanted £20 for 1,000 Scotch firs that he said were only worth £10, leading him to be late with his report, signed on 7 May 1802 in Leith. Having retreated back to the east, he had distance between himself and the management committee when they read that work done by McArthur, Buckie and Gray amounted to £34,226.1s.0½d.

It is perhaps essential to keep in mind that although Rennie was becoming a name to be reckoned with in the canal world, Paterson had had to be sent to England just to see a canal and had been given a few months' hands-on training. And although in England contractors and teams of workmen – so-called 'navvies' – were gaining expertise in this field, the west of Scotland did not necessarily have either companies or workers with the know-how to carry out a complex piece of engineering like this. It is also essential to at least consider why, on 14 September 1801, Paterson had written from Leith to Neill Malcolm in a letter about supplying Mr Malcolm with a lime kiln (a questionable negotiation in itself) about 'Roman Cement'. This is the very stuff that was lacking to make Dunardry Lock watertight, so this makes puzzling reading:

There are 30 casks of Parker Glass Roman Cement lying in a cellar here all marked B.S. which strikes me as belonging to the British Society. The person now in whose possession it lies is John Kay and the expense of freight from London and other expenses is £7 or £8. You will probably know if the society are [*sic*] sending any of that cement to Scotland and on that account I trouble you with this.

It could simply have been that Mr Malcolm had dealings with the British Society and therefore could put in a good word to obtain these 30 casks of pozzolana, but Paterson's postscript seems to contradict that theory, reading: 'If I can be of any use in forwarding the cement or otherwise I shall be ready at your desire.' This seems to make it clear that this was Roman Cement for Mr Malcolm (possibly for his new lime kiln), not for leaky Lock 11. Why would a man working as engineer on the canal tell Mr Malcolm this? If this vital material was available, why was it not bought up and delivered to the contractors working on the Crinan Canal's many structural problems? Mr Malcolm was certainly not a contractor and these are difficult questions to answer. We shall see as this story unfolds that John Paterson's modus operandi was, to say the least, unconventional and this is perhaps an example.

According to Peter Cross-Rudkin in his paper *Canal Contractors 1760–1820,* canal construction involved a number of distinct aspects, which we are beginning to recognise in the unfolding of the Crinan Canal story. The professionals included those involved in the areas of excavation and puddling, the building of locks, bridges and aqueducts, tunnelling, and carpentry in lock gates and bridge and tunnel centres. Cross-Rudkin explains that for much of the canal era, contractors offered to undertake one trade only, and companies organised their works accordingly. The structure of the Crinan Canal management was, at the top, like most others: a company whose shareholders had elected a management committee, who were expected to take a hands-on role in the supervision of construction. The Crinan management, however, faced two major difficulties. Like most management committees, they had cash-flow problems when it came to paying contractors. Unlike most management committees, this wasn't simply about the lack of coinage circulating in the late eighteenth and early nineteenth centuries: the Crinan Canal was dipping into an already empty bucket.

Cross-Rudkin says, 'a contractor without the capital to tide over the problem of shortage of funds would dismiss his workmen'. By the time money was available to get on with the job, the contractor and his workers might have taken on other work. Add to that the fact that the contractors employed by the Crinan Canal management committee seem in the main not to have had the expertise of the teams that at that time were creating masterpiece canals in England, and it is little wonder that matters were getting out of hand. They did have John Rennie heading the operation (when he wasn't too busy elsewhere) and while he insisted that clients should make proper payment if they expected to get good workmanship from their contractors, the problem may well have been that expectations of the contractors were far too high.

Rennie knew that Thomas Telford was someone who could help him get the Crinan Canal back on track and, as the records for June and September 1803 told the same tale of repair after repair after repair, Rennie decided to bring him in on a consultant basis. In 1801, Telford had been contracted to survey for a canal through the Great Glen (which would become the Caledonian Canal). James Watt had been asked by the Commissioners of the Forfeited Estates to do a survey back in 1773 and he had reported that it was practicable, although he commented that it was 'the wildest country I ever saw, and over the worst constructed roads'. Then John Rennie was consulted in 1793 and prepared some plans. By that time, the threat of foreign conflict was a reality and by 1801 the Napoleonic Wars were creating a demand for inland ship canals throughout Great Britain to enable shipping to travel without threat from French privateers – the merchant ships employed in the conflict.

The so-called Great Glen canal was also deemed important in this pre-steamship era to allow vessels to beat the winds and tides prevalent around the coast of Scotland. Vessels from the east coast ports had to struggle through the Pentland Firth on their way to America, and were more often than not port-bound between January and April. It was conjectured that 500 miles of dangerous navigation past the Orkneys and Cape Wrath could be avoided if a shipping canal could be constructed through the Great Glen.

So it was that in 1801 Telford (by then seen as the man to go to for canal construction) was asked for yet another survey, and, after some correspondence with Watt and Rennie, Telford came up with a plan and was asked to go ahead as principal engineer. Rennie made use of the fact that Telford was now working in Scotland and called on him for advice on the myriad problems besetting the Crinan Canal. And so, according to Rennie's Number 2 on the Crinan project, John Paterson, in September 1803 we find Telford 'on his way to Fort William', making a detour in order to inspect the Crinan operation. Telford left Paterson with a lengthy report, asking him to pass it on to the management committee.

There had, in fact, been a series of reports made by not just Telford but also Rennie and Thomas Simpson, the surveyor employed by the management committee at this time. Paterson was to draw on these for his October 1803 report to the management committee in Inveraray. Paterson claimed at one point not to have had access to some of these. In view of his subsequent behaviour, it is tempting to suggest that this was more by design than accident, but that is to condemn a man without full evidence two centuries after the event.

It was Lock 11 at Dunardry that was of most concern, as it was near collapse. The management committee, although charged with that 'hands-on' role in the supervision of the construction, had made it clear that the members didn't feel themselves competent to judge the causes of the problem and that the matter had to be left to the engineers. Rennie and Paterson were to 'lose no time in reporting what should be done'. It seems that the side of Lock 11 was coarse open gravel. There had always been concerns about the site and there had been instructions to the contractor to put a puddle (clay or the like mixed with water and tempered, and used as a waterproof lining for the walls of canals and ditches – pozzolana would, of course, have been more than ideal for the job) under the upper wing walls of the lock. The costs had been considered prohibitive without some kind of trial to see if this would solve the problem. And, of course, three or four months after the opening of the canal, leaks had started to occur. A repair carried out by Mr John Aird, one of the contractors, in October and November 1801 had held for nine months, but by June 1803, the problem was back.

By then, Paterson certainly found it difficult to judge

exactly what was going wrong – the patches on patches were confusing. He suggested observing whether loss of water increased when the lower gates were shut and the lock was filling up. Thomas Simpson, the surveyor who had first noticed a recurrence of leakage in 1 June 1803, wrote on 9 September that 'Lock 11 is still standing' but he was 'apprehensive' that it could not hold out for long as the waste from the bottom of the recess was as great as ever. Paterson commented that he couldn't judge from either Simpson's report or Telford's the precise course of the water that had done the damage. His own first comment was that the puddle (the clay lining intended to create a leak-proof surface) had been 'wasted'. He wanted to see if the leak increased as a result of shutting the lower lock gates and filling up the lock, in which case a break had occurred in the puddling.

Telford's inspection report said that an inverted arch in the upper chamber of the lock was in good order, proving to him that the water had not passed under the body of the building. He explained what he would have done in June, when the leak first reappeared: grooved sheeting piles driven across the lock near the point of the gates and returned upwards to cover the upper corner of the recess completely; removal of damaged timber; repair of the inverted arch in the lower chamber where it had fallen down. But it was clear that Telford was of the opinion that they were closing the lock gates after the boat had sailed. This cannot be interpreted as anything other than a reproof:

> Had this been done at the time the leak made its reappearance in June last, I am very much inclined to believe that the lock would have been in good order . . . and the

disagreeable measure of taking down the masonry, which seems now to be considered necessary, might have been avoided.

He added with biblical conviction, 'This lock has been founded on sand and the foundations have not been sufficiently secured.' And he was in no doubt but that 'the mischief' could not be removed 'by any partial means'. The lower gates and sills would have to be removed immediately to allow the foundations of the walls of the lock to be carefully examined.

His bleak reassurance that 'if they are not undermined they may be perhaps secured and kept up' didn't please Paterson, however. He chose to comment negatively on the expert's advice – Telford's plan could 'not be carried out without taking down the building'. But then it becomes clear in Paterson's October report that he doesn't have any more expertise than the committee itself, engineer or no. He also seems to have been a somewhat petulant man who, despite having been charged with giving the committee Telford's report, expressed annoyance at a lack of information, claiming only to have extracts from Telford's and Simpson's reports that left him in the dark, and throwing a negative light on all he did not agree with. And on 5 October 1803, he defied the respected Telford's advice, given after bothering to take that detour on his way to Fort William to look after the somewhat bigger canal venture currently under his direction. Paterson told the management committee that instead of the major examination recommended by Telford it would be better to 'keep the water in its place'. He expanded: 'Repairing the Arch in the lower chamber where it has been damaged is all I should think necessary.' And he put in a rider to safeguard himself, claiming, 'Mr Telford . . . does not condemn any part of it [the building] without a trial except the inverted arch and the lower chamber of the lock.'

But if the committee was expecting some sort of plan, some sorting out of the various opinions, they had the wrong man in Paterson. Having on the one hand said that minimal work (repairing the lower chamber arch) needed to be done, he then went back to Mr Simpson's comments, calling them 'much more decisive' than Mr Telford's. Decisive? Certainly doom-laden: Simpson said the building could not last much longer. Paterson was a reed blowing in the wind, not really knowing what should be done next, very aware that the budget was tight, and perhaps – despite an increasing arrogance – feeling guilty because he should have blown the whistle some considerable time previously. The clearest part of his report of October 1803 states that 'too many partial attempts' had been made to cure the problem of Lock 11 since it first occurred two years before, and he apologised for not telling Mr Rennie 'before this' in order to 'remedy the evil'. But note that this is not an apology for not having repaired the work, simply for not having told Mr Rennie sooner what a state matters had reached. On the premise that the best defence is a good offence, Paterson attacked Simpson.

Simpson had said in his own report that this was an edifice built on sand (confirmed by Telford). He said that planking had been put down and 'puddle that was washed away' had been replaced with the 'best clay [underlined] that could be got, beat together amongst the piles with little rammers as they could not use large ones'. The contractor Aird had added, 'it was as tight as any lock in the Crinan Canal when I left it'. Paterson told the management committee, 'Notwithstanding therefore of Mr Simpson's strong averment that the recess wall is founded on sand, I must be of opinion that he is wrong.' He twisted the knife with the comment that Simpson and Aird's repairs had not gone deep enough to 'discover the piles'.

Recommendation? Repair as necessary! Hardly a measured opinion based on the evidence of experts. His parting shot to the committee was that he would have gone and done it himself had he not been working in Leith.

If we are to talk of the disasters waiting to happen, we cannot limit ourselves to the failures of construction and the effects of storms. Paterson himself was nothing short of disastrous in his role as engineer and increasingly as unpredictable as the Argyll weather. Not surprisingly, the same issues dogged the progress of the canal over the winter and into the spring of 1804, when, on 6 April, Paterson submitted yet another six-monthly report. In modern terms of monitoring and evaluation, these reports at first sight seem to do little more than pay lip service to the concept – but the contents were, as we shall see, being stored in the heart of Colonel Graham, the clerk to the management committee.

It is possible that Paterson by this time was ill – either mentally or physically – and stressed by awareness of his own incompetence and double dealing (remember that Roman Cement deal). Or perhaps (an unsubstantiated theory this author puts forward based solely on the evidence of the correspondence viewed) he was drunk when he wrote this particular report. He makes no apologies for accusing others of such folly. Certainly, his handwriting was very different and it and the content of the report intimate a disturbed frame of mind. He told the canal management committee that he was concerned for his own character, as well as 'for the welfare of the canal'.

In the age of the television soap opera, we could only call this a cliffhanger and speculate until the next episode. But this was a major engineering project, involving private funds, a government mortgage and the reputations of respected individuals in the canal world. Could one man ruin the whole project? Could the accusations he made in this report be true?

7

The fruits of incompetence

Thomas Simpson, the surveyor, had clearly not been an ally of John Paterson for some time and had evidently attempted to sort out the mess the engineer had allowed to develop. After Paterson had submitted his 'dodgy dossier' at the beginning of October 1803, the management committee had quite rightly asked for clarification from those mentioned in it. Thomas Simpson's counter-report, dated 18 October 1803, employs an interesting use of language. Paterson, he says, 'seems inclined to attribute . . .' and 'Mr Paterson says he would have recommended . . .'. This reads as gentlemanly backstabbing and may have led to Paterson's strange 1804 correspondence.

Simpson is at pains to point out that he has been mentioning faults in the construction of Lock 11 for some time in his reports. He had told the committee, for example, that he had long recommended that the upper sill would eventually need to be lined to prevent a passage for the water to form 'below the building of the lock'. For the record, he says:

> For this purpose Mr Paterson says that instructions were given to the contractor to put a puddle under the upper wing walls of the lock that the lining might have been

joined to when it was found requisite and what was to have been joined to holding ground or rock in the other parts of the pond.

But if the whole damages which have so frequently happened at this lock had been wholly occasioned by the water from the upper pond (which from repeated observation I very much doubt) could not water have been prevented from passing under or behind the building by the puddle which Mr Paterson says the contractor was instructed to put under the upper wing walls being carried wholly across the lock or properly joined to holding ground in the bottom?

And if so why was it not done?

Simpson felt it would all have been a matter of digging to a proper depth to secure the whole thing. Paterson had claimed to be in the dark because he had not seen all the correspondence, yet Mr Simpson had had sight of letters between the contractor Aird and Colonel Graham, the clerk of the management committee. These showed Aird had carried out a series of repairs, but Simpson points out in his own rebuttal, 'although there was a repair it didn't work and Aird didn't ever determine where the water came from'. Simpson was 'rather of the opinion' that the 'mode of repair' John Paterson had then said he would have recommended would not have 'proved effective'.

Simpson wrote:

For as it is evident that the mischief was more owing to the water springing from the bottom of the recess than coming from the upper pond, I can hardly imagine that the piling he speaks of would in any degree have prevented its effects and when in the month of July last the banking was removed from behind the recess on the west or south side of the lock, nothing was observed to justify an opinion of the water having in any great degree formed a passage behind the building.

There's more, but rather than being helpful in unravelling what may really have caused such a disastrous situation at Lock 11 (and disastrous it proved to be in terms of the future stability of the canal) Mr Simpson's remarks in the main seem simply to be part of the warp and weft of a tapestry of incompetence at all levels.

Mr Simpson does, however, make it very clear that Paterson was shuttling in and out of this tapestry, making insinuations designed to put himself in a good light and to do down others. He says:

> Although it is hardly necessary at this time to take any notice of the observations made by Mr Paterson on Mr Telford and my reports, a great part of which in my opinion being of very little consequence and might have been spared, I shall take the liberty of adding a few remarks on them . . . as some of the contents of these reports seem to have been misunderstood by Mr Paterson.

He explains that Telford had to make an informed judgement after just a five-hour inspection of Lock 11. He had, therefore, combined what Simpson told him with his own observations, which 'to a person of his known abilities and experience, was fully sufficient to enable him to judge of the nature of the foundations'. So whatever Paterson thought of Telford, Simpson was impressed enough by his credentials to trust his judgement. Simpson had a further dig at Paterson about the sandy foundations:

> I am satisfied that so far from being brought there in the manner Mr Paterson has stated it was in reality the original sand of the foundation which had never been removed and from which I am certain that the puddle in the bottom of the recess was never joined to that in the back part nor even carried through below the foundation of the walls.

Not only that, but, he continues:

> I am certain of my being correct in saying that no pile was ever placed under the great counter point further than that which supports the hollow – as a great part of the building of the counter point was with much difficulty kept from sinking during the time the building was removed and the great waste under its foundation made up with puddle from outside.

Pots may be calling kettles in all of this, but one thing we can be sure of: the Crinan Canal was in trouble, and weaknesses outweighed strengths at every level.

Simpson told the management committee:

> However unfavourable Mr Paterson's opinion may be of the different attempts lately made to effect a radical cure of the defects of the lock, I have to say that they have been always conducted to the best of my judgement so far as local circumstances would admit.

And, of course, geology was in its infancy. From Watt's first survey in 1771 through to this first decade of the new century, no one had much of an idea from day to day, hour to hour, of 'the nature of the ground', as Mr Simpson describes it. It would have been useful if Paterson had at least talked him through the difficulties that had been faced and how the problems at Lock 11 first occurred. But as Simpson told the management committee, he hadn't been given 'the smallest information on any of these particulars during the time of his [Paterson's] residence at the Canal after my appointment to my present office'. Paterson preferred to spend his time in Leith and that's where he was when he had so unprofessionally suggested he'd have done the repairs himself if he'd been at the canal.

This kind of interdepartmental strife, this bickering about who did what and when, this buck passing and naming and shaming are, of course, only too familiar to us two centuries later. Today, we do it by text and email, but we can see from these wordy letters and reports that this engineering project was threatened not only by lack of cash and all the problems that geology and meteorology could throw at it – but also by poor middle management and staff disputes. It should not surprise us, therefore, to learn that John Paterson's report to the management committee, written on 6 April 1804 at Dunardry, with a copy to the surveyor sent on 14 April, reflects a man under pressure, a man not quite in control of the project or of himself.

Paterson now sought to shift the blame not onto his colleagues, or indeed onto the master canal-maker Telford, but to point the finger at a humble lock keeper, whom he accused of selling liquor and thereby contributing to the disaster that was Lock 11. He told the management committee that while a lock might be 'very well designed, and very well executed' (so no longer blaming Rennie, Aird, Simpson et al) it could then be 'afterwards materially injured or wholly destroyed by improper or unskilful management'. Pompously, he says, 'laying down this as first principle, it follows that person having charge of locks ought among other things to know, that continuing a pressure of water on the lower gates, longer than is absolutely necessary for passing the trade, is improper and may prove highly injurious to the work'.

Now comes the most bizarre turn of Paterson's blame game. He writes:

> It will likewise be granted that lock keepers ought to be of sober and industrious habit and they should be prevented from selling any kind of intoxicating liquor.
> The keeper of Lock 11 has been allowed to sell liquor, and to that circumstance do I attribute much of what has happened to it.

He has taken ten months to work this out. He refers back to June of 1803, when he had stopped vessels sailing through the canal because of the damage at Lock 11. Some vessels waiting to go through the canal had set off round the Mull of Kintyre. Meanwhile, the repair of Lock 11 began and Paterson says (which doesn't appear in his report of the previous October) that 'the earth had been dug out from behind the recess wall to a considerable depth on a Saturday'. The next day, a day when the God-fearing would not have been working and certainly not drinking alcohol, 'a person of the name of McLachlan (who navigated one of the vessels at Crinan, loaded with slate and drawing . . . eight feet water) came with some of his friends and drank at the lock-keeper's house and on Monday morning an order was sent to Crinan for the admission of his vessel to the canal, but prohibiting any other'. Paterson goes on to claim that this vessel did indeed pass through the canal, going through Lock 11 'when the ground was dry'.

Could hung-over Captain McLachlan have got his slate-laden vessel through a dry lock? Paterson claims there were about four feet of water behind the recess when the boat went through 'and it would have been noways [sic] surprising to me that this occasioned the ruin of the lock. That it did not is a strong evidence of the superior quality of this construction'.

Paterson claims McLachlan then made his way to Ardrishaig, where the other 'shipmasters' were understandably annoyed that his vessel had been allowed through when theirs were not.

The engineer doesn't stop there. He declares without a blush that subsequent investigation brought to light that 'it was common for vessels, especially those passing northwards, to remain much longer in the lock with the lower gates shut than there was any occasion for'. The vessels sat for more than an hour in the lock, their masters, according to Paterson, 'generally drinking in the keeper's house'. And 'so general did this conduct become, that a person unconnected with the canal told me he took the liberty of mentioning it to the keeper, suggesting to him the danger which the lock was exposed to on that account'.

And here comes the *coup de grâce*. Having blackened the name of the lock keeper, Paterson now turns to the surveyor: 'What renders this conduct the more extraordinary is, that this house has till lately been the chief residence of Mr Simpson, the company's surveyor.'

To prove his connection between strong drink and a leaking lock, Paterson adds, 'the lock was as tight as any on the Crinan Canal till sometime after the sale of drink commenced. What has happened since is too well known to require a relation from me.'

It is here that he claims that his concern for 'the welfare of the canal, a regard for my own character, and the character of those with whom I acted in the construction of the works' was apology enough for mentioning these 'instances of misconduct'. He planned another report in which he would mention 'several instances of management which appear to me to have been very injurious, and I shall do this with greater freedom, that in several of them I am uninformed to whom they may eventually apply'.

Paterson told the management committee that the lock would soon be in working order, that justice should be sought, and that another keeper should 'be sent to attend to this and the other locks near it, for such a length of time as that it may be seen whether the repair is likely to prove permanent'. And he finished with a flourish, hoping he was not being too 'presumptuous' in recommending a man named Weir who was then keeper of the locks at the Point of Ardrishaig.

Again, Simpson was required to respond and, on 1 May 1804, he put pen to paper. He said that the accusations about the selling of strong drink were 'palpably erroneous' and 'in the highest degree inconsistent with the truth'. He demanded to know if there was evidence of liquor being on sale prior to October 1801, when the leaks were first experienced. Consistent with what is gathered from the reading of all these reports in retrospect and with the objectivity granted by more than 200 years, Simpson makes what seems to be a killer point himself: in October 1803, Paterson had attributed different failures at the lock to natural causes. What had led to Paterson's latest ideas, Simpson admitted he was 'unable to conjecture'.

The surveyor questioned the story of the vessel being allowed through Lock 11 after it had been drained. Three vessels had gone through *before* it was drained, without incident. He said there was no chance of the quantity of water suggested by Paterson getting behind the recess wall. But setting all that aside, Mr McLachlan had apparently off-loaded his slates at Crinan because he was taking his boat to Greenock for repairs. He wasn't taken through a dry canal – and there were no boats at Ardrishaig that night. Simpson himself had told Mr Campbell, the toll collector at Ardrishaig, of the interruption to navigation and no boats passed. As to the drinking, Mr Simpson said the lock keeper was away with his wife that day and didn't return until evening, and when he stayed at the lock keeper's cottage, he had never witnessed any exchange of liquor. And no, it had never been Simpson's main domicile.

Also in the lock keeper's favour was Simpson's avowal that he had never given the 'smallest encouragement' for any boat to stay in the lock longer than necessary. Simpson says, 'the charges advanced by Mr Paterson, which in a collective view I cannot help considering as a shallow artifice to acquit himself and his co-adjutors [*sic*] of all blame in the failure of this lock and thereby in the most unmanly manner, endeavouring to attach to others that which properly is chargeable to himself'.

We might think, 'He would say that, wouldn't he?' But this farcical episode, more fanciful than anything Neil Munro ever thought up for his puffer captain Para Handy, was supposed to have taken place four months after Paterson's October 1803 report was submitted. That had been a fairly blameful but essential technical report, with no mention of any such shenanigans. Surely, this grants Simpson the higher moral ground. The lock was in a mess long before this tale was supposed to have been played out, and while the lock keeper at Dunardry had indeed been granted permission to sell liquor, Simpson reckoned that 'the charges in his report are in the highest degree frivolous and improper'.

The canal was in operation again from 25 April 1804, with the repairs at Lock 11 'proving effectual'. Mr Paterson continued to be somewhat ineffectual, as we shall see.

8

Towards a takeover

None of this ridiculous in-fighting was taking place in an Argyll bubble away from the prying eyes of the world. The management committee could only have been highly embarrassed by the exchanges that were being fed to them as 'reports' because these were, of course, the evidence of the canal's status required by Scotland's Lords Barons of Exchequer and the British government – and indeed the subscribers who had put their faith in the prospectus back in 1793 and allowed the construction of the canal to go ahead. Each of these bodies was owed considerable sums of money. The canal management committee had to prove it was competent despite the engineering setbacks it was faced with. To have such documents as Paterson's April 1804 report scrutinised could have proved far more of a risk to closure of the project than lack of canal dues and leaking locks.

The Crinan Canal had 'opened' on Friday, 18 July 1801, in that this was the first day that a paying vessel had gone through. The revenue for the first year, to 30 June 1802, amounted to £619.18s.6½d. A letter sent to Mr Henry Jardine for the information of the Lords Barons of Exchequer on 6 July 1802, by the canal accountant Mr John Ferrier, explained that although the canal had opened the previous year, 'a great deal remained to be done to complete it'. With hindsight, we can only wonder at this monumental understatement given at the start of the nineteenth century. It would be difficult to match in the decades to come.

The original subscription of £100,000 was 'exhausted', the £25,000 borrowed from the public purse was 'exhausted', and Mr Ferrier explained that the canal would have remained unfinished and 'allowed to go to wreck' if some of the proprietors had not come forward with a new subscription of nearly £10,000. This, with the first year's canal dues, had been spent on the canal, and there were debts at the end of that first year amounting to at least another £10,000. The fear was that if the lenders asked for their money back and took the canal tolls, there wouldn't even be a fund for the repairs needed to keep the work already done in good order.

By January 1803, Colonel Graham, the management committee clerk, submitted a document showing debts of £42,105.18s.5d. Mr Ferrier was writing again to Mr Jardine for the information of the Lords Barons of the Exchequer, 'to enable their Lordships to make up their reports on the subject [of the Crinan Canal] to the Lords of the Treasury'. It doesn't bear imagining the reaction of the Barons of the Exchequer and the Lords of the Treasury if the following year they had got wind of the canal engineer's ravings along with the ever-spiralling debts and continued requests to bail out the project. The fact that over two centuries later the reports remain on file suggests that Mr Graham couldn't bury them, but it is likely that Thomas Telford's drawings and reports were more prominently placed before the eyes of the men with the money.

Telford involved his well-respected collaborator William Jessop in his appraisal of the Crinan Canal's problems. The pair was by now heavily involved in preparing a line for the Caledonian Canal. Jessop visited the Caledonian Canal site in October 1803, so he presumably made that detour to Crinan with Telford on their way to Fort William. Certainly, the eminent engineers both put their names to the suggestions for the smaller canal's rescue plan. In a letter of 8 February 1804, Telford had proposed building a pier at Ardrishaig wholly of rubble, sand and gravel to save £1,000. He advised sand and gravel at Lock 9, saying that one end of the summit 'needs care'. He noted that the bank at Bellanoch Bay should be raised at a cost of £500. There had always been vacillation over the route the canal should follow at Bellanoch. The banking had caused problems from the outset, but the alternative would have been to cut the canal out of the solid rock, round by the head of the bay, destroying the village of Bellanoch. The mindset of the day would probably have shrugged its shoulders at the loss of the village, but the additional cost of between £8,000 and £10,000 would have added to already horrendous debts. We have seen that extra moss had already been placed here and another £500 worth was being advised by Telford.

Dated 24 May 1804, and entitled 'The Report and Estimate of Mssrs Jessop and Telford', it incorporates Telford's report on Locks 9 and 11 and Bellanoch Bay, and there were additional recommendations for the pier and sea wall at Ardrishaig. Another £500 was estimated for wooden defenders for rocky parts of the canal, with which Paterson (still seeing himself as more competent than Great Britain's top engineers) disagreed. The Telford–Jessop recommendations amounted to £12,787, but they suggested that if the work was carried out properly, savings could be made.

Paterson sought more improvements and highlighted

waste and industrial theft in his July 1804 report. A twenty-first-century finger would by now have been pointed at Paterson, with the directive, 'You're fired!' But he was clinging on and flinging mud at both the management and the workers. He wanted the heads and tails of all the locks to be finished with an 'arming of stone', a task that could be done by the keepers 'in slack times as should many other small jobs'. He reported casks of cement that had been sent from Leith back in 1801 that had been 'left to spoil', and dredging machinery that had been 'left exposed in the open fields'. This latter was worth, he said, around £200. He complained that Daniel Thomas, lock keeper at Dunardry, and Duncan Robison, a carpenter, had known that a scam was being operated with materials belonging to the company for the improvement of houses that had become the property of the company. Some had been sold; some had disappeared into 'private use'.

If these were indeed the facts, then Paterson was quite right in citing this as 'another instance of neglect' and cost to the company. But when he says there was no reasonable excuse why lock gates and drawbridges had not been painted to preserve the timbers because 'the materials have been in the custody of the company's servants for about 18 months', surely this is another instance of buck passing? As the man in charge of overseeing the project, was it not his job to make sure these tasks were carried out and to secure company property? It was never his fault, however. He couldn't believe, he wrote in that July report, that renovations of houses had not been authorised by the committee, as people at Crinan had told him. 'On this account I conceive that this neglect must be chargeable to some official servants of the company.'

Yet another swipe at the management committee that would not have read well under the scrutiny of the Treasury was Paterson's assertion, 'I am sorry to say I never saw the interest of a company, or of an individual, under more injudicious management.'

He signs off his 21 July 1804 report in a way that suggests he had become, if possible, even more self-important than his rejection of the Jessop-Telford report already affirmed. He challenged the management not to make him a scapegoat 'after all the instances of misconduct and neglect I have pointed out . . . all of which will be evident to any person who will take the trouble of inquiring into them'. His final scathing prediction was that 'such mismanagement' could only threaten future work 'in the manner Lock 11' had been damaged.

Mr Graham, clerk to the committee, was obviously itching to point that 'You're fired' finger, as is made clear in his 'observations' on Paterson's report in a document dated 23 July 1804, written from Inveraray canal office. The manners of the early nineteenth century were usually far nicer than our twenty-first-century cut-throat world allows – but Mr Paterson would have tried a saint. Mr Graham was a worm who eventually turned.

He wrote:

> I had again to regret that disposition I have for some time past perceived in Mr Paterson to indulge himself in detraction and abuse as well as misinterpretation. In his letters and reports he loses sight of the duty required and expected of him in order to exercise that petulant stile [*sic*] he has thought proper to adopt boldly dealing about him his reflections and assertions without seeming to care whether

he can substantiate them or not and unmindful how a conduct so inconsiderate must injure his own character.

The clerk questioned many of Paterson's assertions. He had, for example, wanted to cut the cost of transportation of timber and lead from Tarbert to Lock 11, claiming it was only 15 miles when in fact it was 20. The road, Graham said, was in parts very bad and the carter should be paid for two days' work – a fair price that Paterson wanted to reduce and for which he had wasted time working out a lower payment. And, of course, such cheese-paring wasn't going to make any useful dent in the debts of the company.

And then there was the contract that said Mr Paterson would visit the canal at least once a year. Graham points out:

> Mr Paterson seeming by no means inclined to look at the Crinan Canal, the Governors and directors in Spring 1803 appointed Mr Telford to visit it and he was accordingly expected, but prevented by other concerns from coming there till August; before which Lock 11 had assumed an alarming appearance but had been repaired by Mr Simpson. On the 20th August 1803 Mr Telford made a report on that Lock, delaying what he had further to say, upon other parts of the works, till his return to the north.

Paterson had, as we have seen, chosen to ignore or 'forget', as Graham puts it marginally more kindly, both Graham's letters and parts of Telford's report and, Graham recorded, wrote an 'angry and impertinent' letter from 120 miles away in Leith. Graham, however, had filed carefully both Paterson's reports and his visits – and the comments, or lack of them, on Lock 11 in particular. But still we find Paterson in his job after

Mr Graham's severe criticisms of July 1804. In a 47-page report submitted on 8 October 1804, the surveyor Thomas Simpson is clearly exasperated that Paterson had questioned the £12,787 estimate Jessop and Telford had submitted. And there is a cruel irony that his 'petulant stile' persists through to 20 February 1805. Some of the many recommendations made by Jessop and Telford in February 1804 were that the banks at Oakfield were too low, banks in other places were leaky and would require puddling, Lock 11 would require considerable expense to make it secure, and of course the need for defenders for the rocky parts of the canal, which Paterson derided as unnecessary.

Then there was a bank collapse at Craiglass burn, halfway between Oakfield and Dunardry. Paterson wrote in February 1805:

> I am therefore decidedly of the opinion that the only safe way of remedying the misfortune is to change the line of the canal, and to place it more westward as marked on the accompanying plan, which alteration may, I think, be compleated [sic] in three months, provided as many men are employed as can work the ground.

No mention that this had been forecast by the experts, just Paterson's Canute-like command to change the very course of the canal.

On 21 February 1805, Mr Graham wrote a memorandum in which he recorded the provision of 25 men, 25 wheelbarrows and six dozen ballast shovels. He suggested that a dam be made on a piece of rock north from Oakfield 'near ground purchased from Campbell of Lettercraigs'. Mr Paterson now disappears from the files, and in his place comes the man most résumés describe as Rennie's right-hand man in the building of the Crinan Canal. James Hollinsworth was certainly an engineer with a good reputation – but John Paterson cannot possibly be airbrushed out of the canal's history. We can better understand the failures of the first few years when we are privy to his colourful contribution.

9

Rescue, disaster and rescue again

Not that James Hollinsworth had a pristine record. He began his career as a mason and had been working in the canal industry since 1787, when he is recorded as a subcontractor on the Oxford Canal. It was there that he built the Dashwood Lock at a cost of £253.12s.8d, and with another contractor built several stone bridges at £50 apiece. He continued working on bridges and tunnels in Oxfordshire, but ran into a spot of bother with our friend William Jessop, who was chief engineer on the Grand Junction Canal and had cause to question Hollinsworth's alignment of the Braunston Tunnel. In this small world of canal construction, Jessop wrote something of a testimonial for Hollinsworth, saying he had never had reason to question his work previously and that he had 'full confidence' in his future work 'as I hardly know anyone that can so well do his duty'. Putting in this word for him saved Hollinsworth from dismissal, but he moved on anyway, going to work on the Kennet and Avon Canal, where the company engineer was, of course, John Rennie.

In 1797, Rennie recommended Hollinsworth for an inspector's post and he was appointed at a very generous salary (which he had negotiated himself) of £150 a year. The following year, he was in trouble for seeming over-payment of contracts and was actually arrested because he said he could not repay the additional sum. Perhaps Rennie felt responsible, having recommended Hollinsworth for the job, but he must also have rated his work because he began to employ him on a number of other commissions. Hollinsworth would do the surveys, so that Rennie could write up the reports. From 1800, Rennie employed him continuously for some 17 years. When he first appears in the Crinan Canal records, he was also heavily involved in building the Royal Military Canal in Kent, planned with the possibility of an invasion by Napoleon in mind. It was a difficult job, requiring the help of two pumps made by Boulton and Watt (which were not delivered because of non-payment) and up to 1,500 soldiers. The major British victory on 21 October 1805 at the Battle of Trafalgar meant this work was not of quite such urgency; indeed, it wasn't completed until 1809, with many question marks hanging over the length of time it had taken to build. By now, however, Rennie had dispatched Hollinsworth to the Crinan Canal, where he was in post until 1811.

The problems we have seen growing to something of a climax on the Crinan Canal in 1804-05 had led inevitably to the maintenance and repairs being halted. The 25 men and 25 wheelbarrows were just about all that could be afforded and a further £25,000 had to be sought before work could meaningfully recommence. This time the bailout came from the Forfeited Estates fund that had evolved from the 1747 Heritable Jurisdictions Act, forcing Highland landowners to accept English rule or forfeit their lands. The canal had effectively been closed from 1804, and the extra £25,000 allowed repair work and reconstruction to continue. With the advance of the money, Rennie was able to re-start the work and he sent Hollinsworth to get on with the job.

The money had not been easily won. With the Duke of Argyll, co-author of the canal, on his deathbed in 1806, his younger brother, Lord Frederick Campbell, Lord Clerk Register for Scotland and one-time MP for Argyll, went almost coronet in hand in April 1806 to the Lords Barons of the Exchequer to explain that debts could not be paid because the canal was not finished and therefore not producing an income. He heavily emphasised the idea that this was a project of national importance (as indeed it was) and pleaded that a meeting to discuss the finances of the canal be postponed until both Lord Lorne (the Duke of Argyll's heir) and Lord Breadalbane, the other author of the original canal plan, could attend. These two gentlemen were required daily at court at the trial of Lord Melville – the last person in the British Isles to be impeached for misappropriation of public money. He was acquitted at this trial, but didn't hold public office again (he had been Home Secretary and First Secretary of State for War).

They called Viscount Melville 'King Harry the Ninth' because he acted the role of king when the real monarch didn't visit Scotland for rather too many years than was wise. It is tempting to think that if the people at the top, like Lord Melville, were suspected of dipping their hands in the public till, it must not have seemed such a big deal when smaller fry deviated from the paths of righteousness. Be that as it may, the barons were convinced to let the Crinan Canal management committee have another £25,000 and Hollinsworth directed the recommencement of work.

In December 1806, two days before Christmas, Hollinsworth's report was far from full of festive cheer. On the one hand, an excess of water was causing banks to collapse. On the other, a lack of water meant the canal didn't have enough water in it to sail a fishing boat. Hollinsworth said that since the canal had reopened in July there had actually been sufficient water simply because 'it has been almost continual rain'. He pointed out, however, that 'had the same season been as dry as it was the autumn before, there would not have been water to pass the little trade there has been'. The old difficulty with leaks was clearly still causing huge problems, because to repair them meant draining the precious water in the canal. And, of course, the aim was to raise the level of water in the canal to 11 or 12 feet. This, Hollinsworth pointed out, would mean that 'all these difficulties will be greatly increased and much more water wanted'.

He stressed, 'it is very evident that what is done, or prepared to be done to the canal, will be of very little use without an ample supply of water'. He proposed, therefore, to make a dam across the glen 'a little above Lini-dow' (the corruption of Gaelic names suggests the English-born Hollinsworth may have had a hard time with the language). He explained that this glen took all the waste water from the lochs above, 'the uppermost of which is Tabrachbuy, Douloch and Carnloch'. These drained into Loch Clachaig and its waste water 'as well as that from Loch Leabatick and Loch Leagater, and the water from all the falling ground to a very great extent comes into the same stream'. He added, 'This water now comes into the canal, and it is of great use, but in heavy rains it comes in such quantities and with such violence that it is a great difficulty to get clear of it without distruction [sic] to the canal.'

He could do away with this 'evil' by making the proposed dam and a sluice to hold back the water. This would create a surface of about 25 acres, 25 feet deep, at the head, diminishing to about eight feet. He foresaw the waste water being taken off into Loch na Feolin by making a cut or drain through the hill – partly through rock. With little expense, he suggested, this could lead to 'the water in Loch Na Feolin [being] raised seven feet', giving a surface of 30 acres. Other lochans above the canal could also have their water levels raised, with drains to take off spare water in heavy rains, preventing the 'difficulty and distruction [sic] of wasting it through the canal'. The drains could double as feeders when the loch was not so full. Still more lochans could be added to this created reservoir, also at 'moderate expense'. Hollinsworth's estimate for this diversion of water to both feed the canal and to prevent the destruction of banking was £1,586.11s. He admitted he wasn't sure of the value of the land that would be incorporated into this network of lochans, but he didn't think the raising of Loch na Feolin would be of much value, as the land at Lochanadd must, he felt, have already been valued, as it was already in use. The land that might be damaged by the drains was also, he thought, 'of little value'.

He suggested in his report: 'Should the company finance not be otherwise adequate to execute the above, I should recommend applying the sum that was allowed for my former estimate for making the graving dock at Portree as this is a thing of much more utility to the canal.' And he added, 'This should be begun without loss of time, so as to save all the water that can be procured for the ensuing summer.' This work went ahead and was in theory an excellent plan. The work on the canal itself also proceeded and by 1809 was considered to be complete.

This was eight long years after Neill Malcolm had received letters at his London home suggesting that Mr Graham was going to travel through the canal on the management committee's own barge prior to being opened to paying vessels. There had been such optimism in 1801 that the canal would make a difference to so many lives. But this first decade of the new century had indeed proved to offer 'the best of times and the worst of times'. Napoleon seemed to be knocking on the door when the canal was first opened, and there were food shortages as a result of the blockades. Mr Langlands, the mapmaker and surveyor, had told James Gow, Neill Malcolm's farming and drainage expert, that when he was in Campbeltown in March 1801 a mob had cut down the mast of a vessel from the Clyde that had come for barley 'because there was no oatmeal in Campbeltown'.

Mr Malcolm was trying to do his bit by updating his agricultural practices, but this seemed to involve the ubiquitous John Paterson to a degree that seems far from appropriate in terms of 'conflict of interest'. Perhaps if he was in a position to organise a lime kiln for Mr Malcolm, there was no harm in that – but why was he buying locks for Mr Malcolm's bedchambers? And far more questionable, why was he giving Mr Malcolm sight of an abstract of the canal company's accounts with all their debts? Yes, Mr Malcolm was a subscriber, but there is no indication that such accounts were shared with the subscribers in Oxford, Birmingham and elsewhere.

There had been optimism that the canal would not only allow ease of maritime traffic but that there would be the opportunity of following through on the exciting ideas proposed by John Knox and his fellow visionaries. There were 450 planned villages founded throughout Scotland between 1725 and 1850. Many of the earlier ones were an outcome of government reaction to the 1715 and 1745 uprisings, when funding secured from the Forfeited Estates was used to create a less feudal society. Others were the creation of landowners seeking to modernise their agriculture, which involved single-tenancy farms and geometrically laid-out villages. By the end of the 1700s, the planned villages began to include those promoted by the British Fisheries Society (including Tobermory and Ullapool).

Neill Malcolm saw the advent of a canal through the middle of his property as an opportunity to lease out some of his lands. His agricultural expert, James Gow, had grander ideas.

Mr Malcolm's own advertisement for the proposed project was quite modest. It would have been distributed in leaflet form, most probably at cattle markets and the like, as, until the first decade of the nineteenth century, newspapers were published only in five Scottish towns – Edinburgh, Glasgow, Aberdeen, Dumfries and Kelso. It was headed 'Long leases and grounds to be feued', and read:

> The proprietor of the great moss of Creenan in Argyllshire having improved and subdivided about 500 acres of it in a substantial manner, and having built thereon a compleat [*sic*] steading of slated farm houses and offices, is desirous to let the improved part, for a term of years, to a farmer who will follow thereon a proper rotation of culture.
>
> Bay of Creenan 3000 acres – a considerable descent towards the sea which facilitates draining it.
>
> The vicinity of the Creenan Canal, which passes through part of this ground, affords as easy conveyance to and from the Clyde; and there is always a ready market in the neighbourhood for every part of the produce of the land, particularly for grain, which is imported annually in large quantities from other countries.
>
> On the inner bason [*sic*] at the west end of the Creenan Canal, contiguous to the above grounds, there are lots to be feued for the building or to be let on leases, renewable at the end of every nineteen years, for ever, on payment of a small premium or grassum [a Scottish legal term meaning

a single payment, often made in addition to a periodic payment such as rent, or any payment made to a landlord by a person wanting to obtain a tenancy].

For particulars . . .

However, the ambitious James Gow saw this instead as an opportunity to create a planned village next to the canal. Writing to his employer on 24 November 1800, he enclosed his own advertisement, admitting, 'I have taken the liberty of deviating considerably from your scroll' and adding, 'You will perhaps be startled at the idea . . .'

Gow's idea is indeed startling. He reckoned to cram 80 houses and 'sufficient lodgings for two hundred and forty families or twelve hundred people' into one acre. The gardens and grazing for these 80 households would themselves, Gow thought, feu at £4 an acre and £2 a cow, 'not to mention the hay necessary to support them over winter which of course must be purchased from your own improvements as well as all other articles of provisions that these improvements can furnish'. In other words, they would all owe their souls to the estate, to paraphrase the old US mining song, which tells of workers being paid in vouchers to be spent only in the company store. Gow had done the maths and worked out that providing 'twelve hundred inhabitants in the single article of meal cannot be estimated at less than 2,200 Bolls and must of course greatly enhance the value of your whole estate'. He thought that within Neill Malcolm's own lifetime (the landowner was then 63) six acres could be settled in this way, consuming 'the produce of your whole estate supposing the moss in the highest state of cultivation'. With a touch of early nineteenth-century sycophancy, Gow told his employer that such a scheme would render his name 'immortal'.

The 'deviation' from Mr Malcolm's original advert was considerable indeed. It begins: 'Lands in Argyllshire to let on long leases; grounds to be feued; a village built, and manufactories established at the west end of the Crinan Canal.' Gow may have had excellent skills in draining land and improving agriculture – he was obviously also a snake oil salesman manqué. Describing the developments to the estate in much more lavish language than his employer had done, he puts out some very tasty bait to attract tenant farms before moving on to the planned village. Here he is more than a little economical with the truth, attributing the idea and indeed plans to Mr Malcolm:

As there is every possibility that the west end of the canal, terminating in the bay of Crianan [yet another spelling to juggle with], will soon become the centre of considerable commerce, the proprietor wishes to promote that object by every encouragement in his power. With this in view, he has sketched out a regular village, and proposes to feu steadings, upon a given plan, at the quit rent of only one penny each annually. Settlers can be furnished with garden ground at a moderate feu; and the daill [meadow] adjacent is of the best quality for the pasturing of cows.

There is an open slate quarry of good quality in the grounds, and a profusion of lime in the neighbourhood.

A dry dock of the best construction is built on the bay, which opens into the great tract, leading from the North of Europe to Clyde, Ireland, and the Western coast of England . . .

There was much, much more extolling the virtues that would develop from this little paradise of a village – including workshops, opportunities for small businesses to set up, and a weekly market. This was all to be compressed into a triangle of land adjacent to the canal. Perhaps the changes of two centuries to the topography of the area have made it difficult to see the potential – but Gow's deviation from Mr Malcolm's gentlemanly proposal smacks of greed and exploitation.

This was a time, however, when 'ordinary' folk could be told to move here, work there, don a uniform and fight an enemy – all without consultation, compensation or very much pay. In his April 1801 correspondence, John Campbell of Prospect Farm, the Malcolms' factor, records the problems of a tenant at Barnakil, whose acre was to go under water to accommodate the canal and who like so many other tenants could not sow 'any part of it'. Campbell's advice was to cut the rent and then claim back from the canal company, and he was 'set against' Neill Malcolm's suggestion to offer the man a new house. Gow's plan to get his proposed villagers to pay through the nose for growing their kale, grazing their cow and buying their oatmeal would have incited no criticism from the Duntroon estate neighbours, who feared for their own livelihoods.

However, not all disrespect of tenants went without censure. John Campbell had given notice of eviction to a number of tenants, including 34 in the settlement of Arichonan (where in 1848 there would be a violent eviction with police involvement). Another John Campbell, the Malcolm lawyer in Inveraray, wrote to Neill Malcolm on 20 March 1801 about the 'vast heap of removings from your property this year'. He had already contacted his namesake at Prospect Farm 'pretty strongly' because, as he told Mr Malcolm, this was 'bad policy as well as oppression'. Warning people (of eviction) when 'not absolutely necessary' was inhumane, he said. 'It banishes all confidence in those that remain and with that all attachment. It amounts to a prohibition of improvements and produces perpetual comprisements [*sic*] of buildings in which the landlord's interest always suffers'.

Although the lawyer's own interests were obviously in favour of his client, this man did have the welfare of the people at heart, too. He was obviously annoyed at the high-handedness of the factor, telling Mr Malcolm, 'If the person superintending it is not free in every interest of prejudice or misinformation it is the source of great injustice and oppression and in a season of scarcity like this it sets whole families that cannot get a place elsewhere abegging.' The food riots in Campbeltown should have been warning enough that people were suffering and could not be chased from one situation and find another easily. Now the lawyer had Mr Malcolm's evicted tenants 'applying to me for a place'. He suggested, 'Perhaps it may not yet be too late to write him [the factor] a caveat', and wondered if some of the 34 from Arichonan would not be accommodated elsewhere on the estate.

The first Neill Malcolm was in ill health in 1801 (he would pass away on 1 April 1802, to be succeeded by Neill Malcolm II) and was struggling to keep up with paperwork. As landowner, he was expected to pay a proportion of the cost of making roads, and this was a decade when, following an Act of Parliament in 1800, new roads and bridges proliferated, particularly to facilitate access to the new canal.

The dawn of the new century must have brought with it hopes and fears, ambitions and assumptions that this was a major step into modernity. But every new century seems to falter in the first decades – wars, food shortages, homelessness, public projects that go awry are stock features in the annals of the early nineteenth, twentieth and twenty-first centuries.

We should, therefore, feel no surprise to learn that even with a new, competent engineer on the job, the Crinan Canal almost didn't make it past the first decade. Hollinsworth's clever proposal to join all the lochans together into one big reservoir to feed the canal was perhaps an idea too far, considering the rainfall experienced in Argyll. In January 1811, another serious incident had to be reported. A heavy gale washed away the principal embankment of the new reservoir at Glen Clachaig and water rushed into the canal, sweeping away part of the road, closing it to navigation. There was serious damage to the lock gates, embankments and other works on the canal summit, which was flooded 'and injured to a great extent'. The canal management committee must have felt like a collective Sisyphus, pushing the progress of the canal towards its goal, only to watch it roll back to a state of chaos and greater debt.

On 16 October 1811, the engineer Robert Stevenson and James Hollinsworth examined 'the whole extent of the canal', according to Stevenson's report to the committee of directors for the management of the Crinan Canal dated 22 October. They concentrated, of course, on the worst damaged section of the canal. It was bad. The history of the creation of the new reservoir was noted and Stevenson wrote:

> This supply was most seasonably felt during the summer of 1810 but in the month of January last, as the committee but too well remember, the embankment of the new reservoir which covered many acres of ground to the depth of 20 feet of water, gave way in the middle, leaving a breach of about seventy feet in the embankment; this immense body of water rushing through a precipitous glen or ravine and carrying everything before it, is described as instantly

filling the summit reach of the canal and the locks on both sides.

Lock gates, walls and basins between locks had been destroyed and the banks imploded, choking the locks from Cairnbaan to Dunardry. This had left, Stevenson said, 'a dreary and destructive waste which but an hour before exhibited the busy scene of commerce, affording a strong example of the wealth and prosperity of a country, but especially of their public spirit which has so eminently distinguished the Crinan Canal Company'.

The saddest thing about this latest disaster was that the canal had for the first time been up and running in the way it had been intended. The words of that 1792 prospectus seemed to be coming to fruition. But now a gale combined to blow high water in the reservoir over its artificial confines. The pressure of so much water couldn't fail to smash the embankment and bring the full force down to the canal below. Improvements were recommended and it was suggested that with a good spell of weather and 'intense work' the canal could be made navigable, although the rest of the canal was not really in good shape. But it was clear that nothing could be done until the summer of 1812 – another year when government money would be tight because of conflict abroad. It was the start of the American war against Great Britain, and of course the Peninsular War was still going on. These world events aside, the company's debts continued to mount and canal workmen had not been paid regularly. An unrealistically low government loan of £5,000 was not enough to repair the immense damage.

New public roads which had scarcely been completed were broken up at Cairnbaan and Daill ('Dell', as Rennie would have it), and there was a need not only of 'intense work' on gates and earthworks, but of 60 feet of oak timber, '12 sticks' of Lochaber timber and 1,695 cubic feet of tar. Pitch pine timber was also needed. Credit of £2,000 and £3,000 was obtained from bankers in Glasgow on the private security of the Duke of Argyll and his brother, who, according to the Revd Alexander Mackenzie, minster of South Knapdale, writing for *The Second Statistical Accounts of Argyllshire,* 'came forward on this occasion to secure the benefit of the former expenditure to the public, and which loan, it is inferred, has been paid by and remains a debt due to [in 1845] the Argyle family'. The estimate to 'render the navigation of the Crinan Canal safe' was £12,752.19s.6d. Stevenson didn't even bother to include two iceboats that would be needed in future for winter operations because he knew there was no chance of them being purchased.

Thomas Telford saw the canal in January 1813 and described it as 'at present in a very imperfect condition'. In his official report, dated 4 March 1813, and addressed to The Right Honourable, The Lords Commissioners of His Majesty's Treasury (the body that commissioned him to write the report) he had to go through the old litany of damaged lock gates, leaks, decayed drawbridges, poorly cut rocks that left the sides of the canal dangerous to vessels – and to add that the summit remained dangerous following the embankment collapse. The work was practicable, he said, but expensive. The estimate now was £18,251, and it was clear that no one was going to make any profit from it. This must have been so frustrating to everyone concerned, and particularly to Hollinsworth, whose hard work had more than doubled the number of passages through the canal.

In 1804, 668 single journeys had been recorded. In 1809, there were 1,168. By 1810, this had risen to 1,578, and even in 1812, the year after the disaster, there were 665 journeys recorded during the periods the canal was able to operate.

Telford told the Treasury:

> From these circumstances, from my own experience of the passage, and the opinions of the best informed persons I have conversed with, I am warranted in saying that the intercourse of that part of the kingdom would be materially injured if this communication was now abandoned and which must be the case unless Government takes it up.

He acknowledged the loans already granted, the debts accruing (from 1799 to 1816, £74,400 was granted through a series of government statutes), and added: 'If therefore it be judged advisable to proceed with the completion of this work the most advisable scheme seems to be to put it under the direction of the Commissioners of the Caledonian Canal.'

And so, the final advance in 1816 was not made to the Crinan Canal management but to the Caledonian Canal Commissioners, who were to administrate the funding, and the canal became government property – in theory until it paid off all its government debts. Telford was to supervise the repairs and he suggested that a realistic £2,000 per annum could be looked for as a clear revenue once the canal was up and running again. This was the start of a new phase in the Crinan Canal's story.

10

New beginnings, old problems

The rescue operation to save the Crinan Canal from closure was, of course, carried out by powerful people in high places and a significant player on this stage was Thomas Telford. Telford had throughout this new century an increasingly important role in the government's major plans to rescue Great Britain itself from social and economic difficulties and to safeguard its international trade. In Scotland, Telford was asked to select the most suitable sites for fishing stations on the west coast, to plan road and bridge communication on and between the mainland and the Islands, and, as we have seen, to look at the possibility of constructing a canal through the Great Glen.

He had reported to the government on 30 November 1801 that an improvement of communications in the Highlands was both essential and feasible, and, he said, an 'intimately connected system' would 'very evidently have a striking effect upon the welfare and prosperity of the British Empire'. Given the go-ahead, he developed a five-point plan in 1802 that included better roads and bridges, development of the Caledonian Canal, promotion of fisheries on both east and west coasts, prevention of emigration, and links between Great Britain and Ireland, with improved road links between Portpatrick

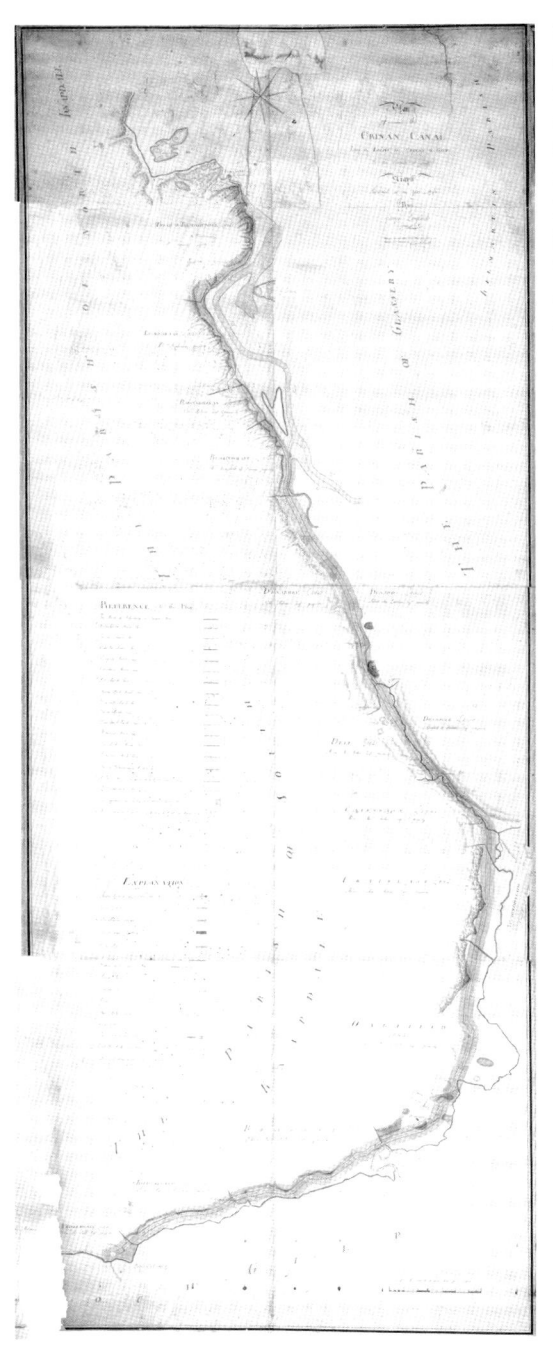

George Langland's map of the canal route from 1794. The cartographer and surveyor was employed by the Duke of Argyll and mapped the canal with his son, Alexander (Scottish Canals collection).

Early 1790s elevation of the Bellanoch section of the Crinan Canal, showing two- and three-storey buildings and a sailing craft (Clare Gent collection, inherited from her father, Terence Gent).

A 1790s elevation of the Craiglass section of the canal where, in 1805, heavy rains would cause a calamitous bank collapse (Clare Gent collection, inherited from her father, Terence Gent).

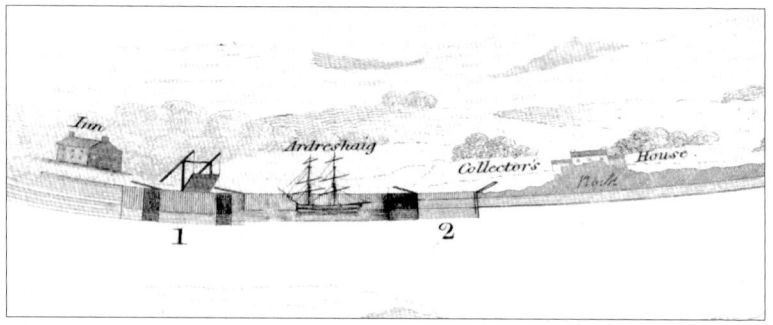

The entrance to the canal at Ardrishaig, Locks 1 and 2, the inn and the Collector's House, with an outcrop of rock marked clearly in front of the building (Clare Gent collection, inherited from her father, Terence Gent).

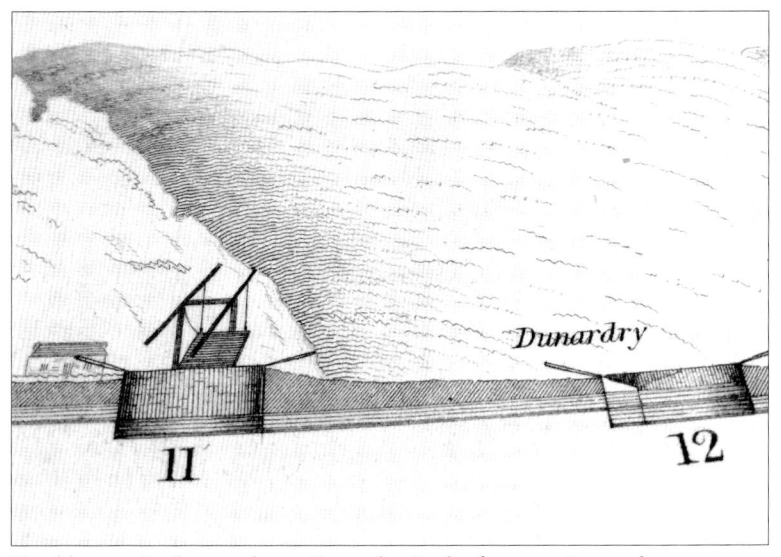

Troublesome Locks 11 and 12 at Dunardry. Lack of appropriate underwater cement would lead to disastrous leaks (Clare Gent collection, inherited from her father, Terence Gent).

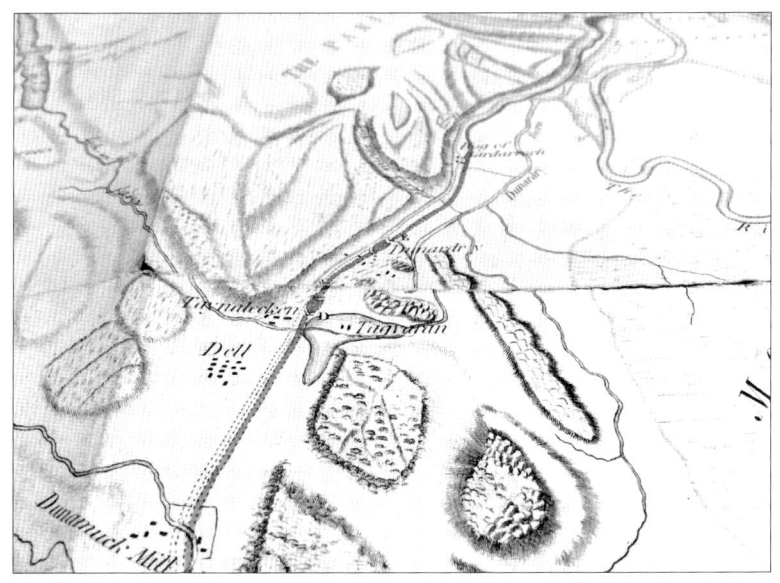

The 'Dell' section of the canal from the 1792 map drawn up by John Rennie for the Duke of Argyll and Lord Breadalbane (Clare Gent collection, inherited from her father, Terence Gent).

This elevation shows a section of the canal where planned rock-cutting is clearly marked. Some 400 men worked on the earliest excavations (Clare Gent collection, inherited from her father, Terence Gent).

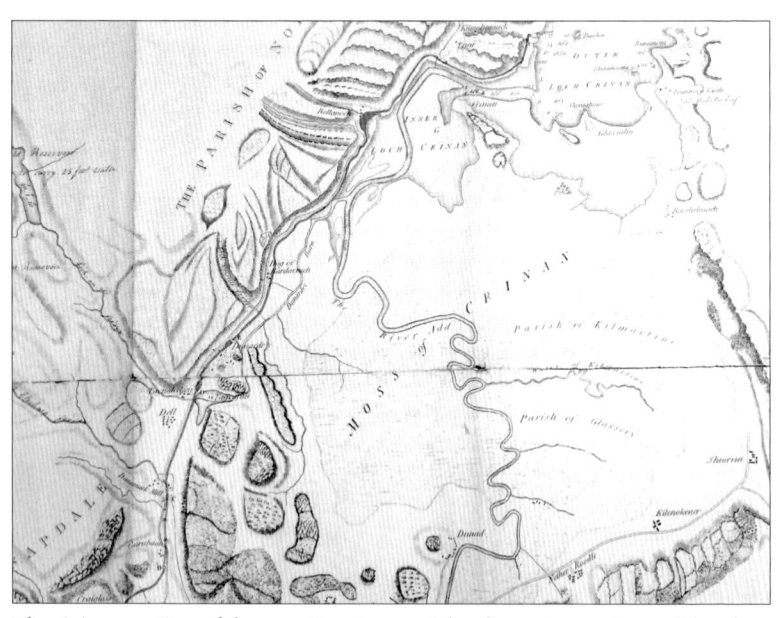

The Crinan section of the 1792 Rennie map. The alternative route considered would have crossed Crinan Moss and exited at Neill Malcolm's Duntrune Castle (Clare Gent collection, inherited from her father, Terence Gent).

By the end of the 1800s, Ardrishaig was a bustling harbour, but the fishing skiffs remind us of the earliest elevations (Duncan MacMillan collection).

As steamers got bigger, passengers transferred at Ardrishaig pier to small craft for transfer to Crinan and their onward journey by steamer to Oban and Inverness (courtesy Argyll Library Services).

In 1847, Queen Victoria and Prince Albert sailed through the canal on a beautifully decorated barge – their 'Royal Route' put the Crinan Canal on the tourist map (Archie Campbell Collection, Argyll and Bute Library Service).

The 1859 disaster destroyed the road and a large part of the canal at Dunardry. The noise of the hillside collapse was heard over five miles away (*Illustrated London News* drawing).

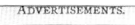

Above. The canal never seemed able to make ends meet, yet thousands of passengers were disgorged every year from steamers landing from the Clyde (Michael Hopkin collection).

Left. James Watt's steam-power developments soon made the canal he surveyed outdated. This poster shows how popular steamer tours became, but the canal was too small for such boats (courtesy Argyll & Bute archives).

Launched in 1866, the much-loved *Linnet* took passengers through the canal for just over 60 years. She is at the end of her career here at Cairnbaan (Michael Hopkin collection).

The *Linnet* going through Lock 9, with her boat shed to the right of the picture (Archie Campbell Collection, Argyll and Bute Library Service).

The cluster of two- and three-storey buildings appearing on the 1790s' elevation of the Bellanoch section had, a century later, become a bustling village, thanks to the canal (Michael Hopkin collection).

A parliamentary inquiry in 1839 questioned (amongst much else) the lack of inns on the canal. Today's hotel at Crinan grew out of one of the few inns that accommodated passengers in the early 1800s (Michael Hopkin collection).

The Glendarroch Distillery moved to the banks of the canal in 1831 from a site in Ardrishaig. The canal's role in enabling industries to flourish was undervalued at Westminster (Michael Hopkin collection).

Towpaths became thoroughfares for crofters and estate workers. Sheep and cattle were herded along the banks of the canal to the market in Kilmichael Glassary and later Lochgilphead (courtesy Argyll Library Services).

The canal was designed for working boats, and although these changed enormously, trading and fishing vessels continued to be its lifeblood through the nineteenth and twentieth centuries (courtesy Argyll Library Services).

The stances at Ardrishaig, where the fishermen mended their nets. Far fewer boats and men were lost once the canal cut out the need to round the dangerous Mull of Kintyre (Duncan MacMillan collection).

A prisoner-of-war camp was built above the canal at Cairnbaan during the Second World War. German and Italian prisoners were held there (courtesy Argyll Library Service).

Loch Fyne became a practice zone for the Normandy landings during the Second World War and the canal saw mini submarine traffic heading out for duty in the Atlantic (Archie Campbell Collection, Argyll and Bute Library Service).

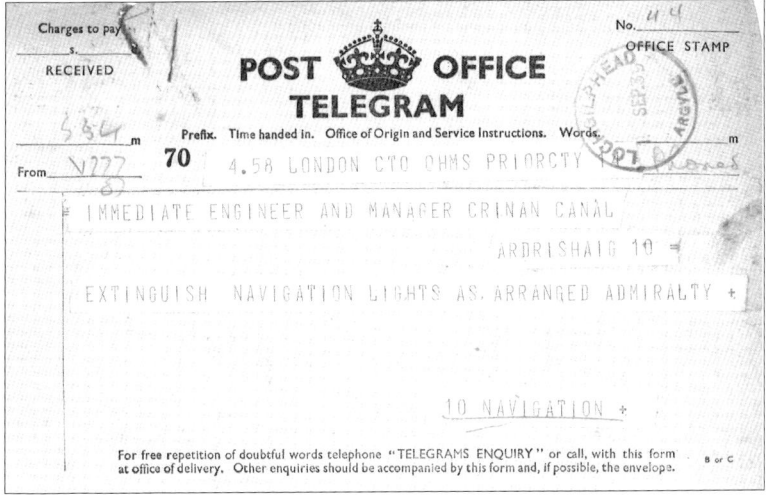

With war imminent, this telegram from the Admiralty plunged the canal (a strategic waterway) into darkness from September 1939 after Germany invaded Poland (Scottish Canals collection).

The lock gates at Crinan lead to the open sea. Fishing and trade with the Western Isles became more viable with the advent of the canal (Karen McCurry collection).

Throughout its history, the Crinan Canal has needed repairs below the water line. Now, the canal is routinely drained for maintenance (Scottish Canals collection).

The 'most beautiful shortcut in the world' offers stunning views at every turn. Lock 14 is no exception (Karen McCurry collection).

Forestry paths take walkers high above the canal and show it at its best, ribboning through the peninsula. This looks down on the Cairnbaan section (author's own collection).

The River Add flows across Crinan Moss into Loch Crinan. Rennie's alternative route, and the late nineteenth-century ship canal plans, suggested a waterway emerging at Duntrune Castle on the far shore (author's own collection).

and Carlisle. As the century progressed, so did Telford's innovative plans. He sub-contracted to the companies he thought best suited to the various works. Knowing this background makes it clearer why the visits he made in the early days to the Crinan Canal really were an enormous favour to Rennie and the ridiculous way in which John Paterson dismissed his advice would today, given the end results, have led to public inquiry.

Now in 1816, the Crinan Canal Commission was to report to the commissioners of the Caledonian Canal, who in turn had government masters to answer to. Both were the property of the government, and funding for the Crinan Canal was to be channelled through the Caledonian Canal commissioners. It was clear that the Crinan Canal continued to be seen as important in the wider plan for an effective infrastructure in Scotland.

At grassroots level, however, the success or failure of the canal meant life or if not death for the men working on the canal, then all too often emigration and severing of family ties. Since the canal construction began, teams of workers had sweated to create this nine-mile tract across one of Argyll's many fingers of land. Lack of funding meant they frequently were not paid, and the lock keepers were no more secure.

When John Paterson lost the plot and accused all and sundry of causing damage to the waterway, one of his main targets had been a lock keeper at Dunardry. We don't know what happened to that poor man and his wife – whether the Ardrishaig keeper recommended by Paterson was given the job in his stead, with its keeper's cottage as part of the wages. We do know that subsistence on the parish was the fate of those out of work. And we know that by 1810 Murdoch Brodie was lock keeper at Kilduskland and that he stayed there until 1813, when he moved to Ardrishaig, presumably to the collector's house, which suggests that he was well trusted. It is almost impossible to imagine how the Brodies managed – Murdoch and his wife Sarah Turner had at least 14 children. The first, Duncan, was born in 1793, the year of the Act that brought the Crinan Canal into being. Although the family's lives were intertwined with the canal, by the time it was under scrutiny yet again in 1832, Duncan's younger brother Robert (born in 1798) and several more of the Brodie brood had left for Ontario.

In the first decade of the nineteenth century, boat after boat transported desperate families across the Atlantic. Typical were three boats that left Tobermory for Canada, each carrying more than 50 adults and 40 children on the six-week voyage. This was before steam, so the journey must have been particularly hazardous. When the American war with Britain broke out, Canada would have to have been the destination for several years.

In August 1819, three laden boats left Oban for Canada, taking 58 days to reach the emigrants' new country. By now, the Highlands were suffering badly from the post-war recession and emigration was haemorrhaging the already thin population. When the Brodies set sail, they were literally and metaphorically a drop in the emigration ocean. On 25 August 1849, *The Scotsman* newspaper reported that 20,000 Highlanders had emigrated to Canada during the previous decade.

The Crinan Canal was struggling throughout this time to become the important link in Highland trade and industry that its original prospectus had promised, and those like Murdoch Brodie and his son George, who became a lock keeper at Dunardry, must have struggled sorely along with it.

George lived with his wife Catherine in the cottage at which Paterson had pointed his accusing finger, calling it the den of drinkers whose behaviour had wrecked the lock. George wasn't born until after that infamous allegation and he lived a long life (from 1808 to 1882), passing away at Dunardry, to be buried along with his parents and, in her turn Catherine, in the graveyard at Kilmory. George worked in a marginally more settled period of the canal's history, but his parents must often have felt the pinch, even though they had a lock keeper's roof over their heads.

Apart from the geological difficulties that the route had presented – and continued to present – to the contractors, and the Argyll weather that was either too wet or too dry to keep the canal operating consistently, 1812 had been a landmark year that introduced the steamship to the Clyde estuary. We have seen that James Watt, having chosen the site and marked out the general route of the canal, removed from the scene to go into a partnership with Matthew Boulton to develop the steam engine in the heart of industrial England. It was frequently remarked upon that the depth planned for the Crinan Canal was shallow, even for vessels prevalent at the end of the eighteenth century. Watt's name is forever linked in a very positive way with the Crinan Canal, but the reality is that the depth and width allowed by his chosen route (endorsed and developed by John Rennie), coupled with his brilliance in developing the steam engine, combined to threaten the very existence of the waterway.

The use of a steam engine to create a paddle steamer that could outstrip any sail-driven vessel was one of the great inventions of the early nineteenth century. PS *Comet*, named after the spectacular appearance in 1811's night skies of what was known as the Great Comet, was built for Henry Bell, who owned a hotel and spa in Helensburgh on the Clyde estuary. When John Wood and Company of Port Glasgow developed his designs, Bell expanded his business empire by publishing this advertisement in the *Greenock Advertiser* in August 1812:

> The Steamboat *Comet*
>
> Between Glasgow, Greenock and Helensburgh for Passengers Only
>
> The subscriber, having at much expense, fitted up a handsome vessel to ply upon the River Clyde from Glasgow, to sail by the power of air, wind, and steam, intends that the vessel shall leave the Broomielaw on Tuesdays, Thursdays, and Saturdays about mid-day, or such hour thereafter as may answer from the state of the tide, and to leave Greenock on Mondays, Wednesdays, and Fridays in the morning to suit the tide.

The *Comet*'s earliest voyages saw her achieving five miles an hour – perhaps not the speed of light connected with its namesake, but impressive against conventional craft. People were keen to pay the four shillings for a first-class cabin and three shillings for second. Nothing stands still, of course, and this plucky little paddle steamer, 45 feet long, with a beam of ten feet and 28 tons in weight, was soon outclassed as competition built bigger and better and faster steamboats that sailed the sea lochs, taking passengers up Loch Fyne to Inveraray. And, of course, by 1819, much bigger and better powered steamboats were crossing the Atlantic. The *Comet* herself was actually able to go through the Crinan Canal, and by 1819 was doing a four-day journey through the waterway to Oban and on to Fort William. Sadly, on 13 December 1820 the *Comet* was wrecked off Craignish Point near Oban, with Henry Bell on board. Fortunately, there were no fatalities. Her eight-year career paralleled a period of transition for the Crinan Canal, but there was no possibility of shoehorning the bigger and better steamboats through the narrow and shallow waterway. The canal was under threat of being left behind by technology developed by the man given credit for her creation.

A parliamentary committee reviewing the history of the canal in 1832 noted (along with all the painful reminders about finance) that the canal was 24 feet wide, about 12 feet deep, and 'is navigable by vessels of 200 tons burden'. It added, 'It is chiefly used by small coasting and fishing vessels, and by the steam-boats which ply between Inverness and the Clyde.' The *Comet* had been well suited to go through the canal, but taking a boat of just 28 tons out into the potentially rough seas beyond Crinan was asking for trouble. Already the steam era was convincing people that this was an ideal way to travel and as the nineteenth century progressed, travelling from Glasgow to Inverness by steamboats via the Crinan and Caledonian canals would become the fastest possible route. But note the plural, 'steamboats': one boat could not make the whole journey because of the narrowness of the Crinan Canal – passengers had to be transferred from Ardrishaig to Crinan before making the onward journey.

Telford must have been very aware of the advantages an improvement of this Glasgow-Inverness route would bring, but after the transfer of the responsibility for the Crinan Canal to the commissioners of the Caledonian Canal reports do begin to reflect a sentiment that the Caledonian Canal (never far from trouble itself) was the more important player and Crinan the Cinderella in the kitchen who might never go to the ball. For 20 years after all administration was put into the hands of the Caledonian Canal commissioners, the story of the first 16 years of Crinan are almost re-run – although without some of the most dramatic episodes provided by wind, weather and John Paterson.

By 1816, the resident engineer was William Thomson, who submitted a report to the parliamentary committee that seems to have made its collective eyes water. The committee had already heard from Mr Caldwell, now secretary to the Crinan Canal Company, who wrote:

> ... not only the whole money raised by the subscribers, being upwards of £88,000, and the tolls and other revenues to the amount of about £15,000, but also the sum of £55,000 which has been advanced at different times by Government, and about £12,000 borrowed on transferable securities and otherwise, amounting in the whole to above £180,000, has been expended on the undertaking; and from a report and estimate recently made by Mr William Thomson, the resident engineer, it appeared to Your Committee that the sum of £19,207 is still wanting to repair and completely finish the works in a secure manner.

As we know, the Crinan Canal Company was not able to repay the £55,000 advanced by the government ('totally unable to raise the above sum' was the rather scathing comment from the parliamentary committee chair), but the advantages to fishing of keeping the canal open won the day and Mr

NEW BEGINNINGS, OLD PROBLEMS

Thomson's request for £19,207 was granted on 13 June 1816. But although the canal was reopened on 20 November 1817 and 20 vessels, towed by horses, passed from Crinan to Ardrishaig that day, it was no kick-start to prosperity. The £19,207 (or £19,400, as it was to be referred to in later inquiries) was a sum to be regarded as a debt due, like the £55,000 still unpaid, to the public purse. The company still owed a substantial amount to the British Linen Bank, wages had risen in the intervening years and the cost of materials (not just gunpowder and pozzolana but timber, gravel, stone and slate) had also increased alarmingly.

We flag up the twentieth century as the one in which technology, science and engineering moved faster than at any point in history — but it is clear when the various parliamentary committees reviewed the history of the canal that no one had expected the advances in shipping that occurred in those first few years of planning and construction. A report in 1804 was cited as saying profits could have been increased if the company had made the canal 'of small dimensions'. The criticism was because the canal company aimed to 'accommodate large vessels engaged in foreign trade': it had increased the construction costs and lowered the revenue by making a bigger canal. Not big enough. Just ten years later, bigger and better steamboats were outclassing the plucky little *Comet* and the canal was too small for the kind of 'foreign trade' that had been expected.

In 1816, John Seton Karr, secretary to the Crinan Canal Company, could only argue that if the canal 'should be stopped and go to ruin for want of further assistance', the fisheries would be deprived of the advantages gained to date and further commerce with the Islands would fail. The grandiose ideas of the canal enabling trade with the Baltic were already eclipsed by a new era of propulsion. Time and again, any commendation of the usefulness of the canal was tempered by the qualification that it would have been better if it were bigger. The alterations, repairs and maintenance carried out always seem to have been make-do-and-mend. There were persistent moves by the original proprietors to have the canal restored to their ownership and efforts were made to raise money to make proper repairs and bring it up to an acceptable working standard – but debt continued to hang over the canal like the sword of Damocles.

However, it was in operation by 1822, and for some time it staggered along under a somewhat haphazard management. By 31 December 1827, £218,936 was owing to an assortment of creditors. After much discussion, negotiation and review, George, 6th Duke of Argyll, wrote from his London home at Upper Brook Street to the Chancellor of the Exchequer, Henry Goulburn, on 21 March 1828, in his capacity as Governor of the Company of Proprietors of the Crinan Canal. He enclosed a draft of a Bill that hoped to relinquish 'the debt due to the public by the Company of Proprietors of the Crinan Canal' in accordance with the various findings of the parliamentary committees. He explained that he had entrusted a petition to the House of Commons to Mr Malcolm junior, one of the directors, 'who has not yet had an opportunity of speaking to you on the subject' but if necessary would attend the progress of the Bill. The letter concludes: 'The Governor and Directors propose, when the Bill shall pass into a law, to borrow money for executing the repairs now necessary on the canal, and with that view have directed an estimate of the expense to be prepared, and transmitted to them from Scotland.'

So, no change there. More money needed, more parliamentary approval needed, more complications in terms of a direct line of management. A Resolution on the Crinan Canal Report was reached in the House of Commons on 17 April 1828 and reported on in the House the following day. The Resolution read: 'That the Company of Proprietors of the Crinan Canal be released from the repayment of the debt due from them to the Crown, and that the same be charged on a proportion of the net revenue arising from the said canal.'

The Resolution was agreed to and a 'Bill for Relinquishing, under certain Conditions, the Debt due to the Public from the Company of Proprietors of the Crinan Canal' was brought in by Mr George Banks and Mr Malcolm. The Bill's conditions were lengthy and catalogued the loans, the progress, the setbacks, the 'extraordinary expense' and the 'national improvement'. The proprietors were to be released of their debt but the proprietors had to carry out provisions for maintaining the canal, for 'securing to the public a proportion of the free revenue in lieu of the sums hereby relinquished', and a fund had to be established for the future maintenance of the canal. Any surplus from the fund and from rates and duties was to be divided between the public and the proprietors in proportions dictated by parliament. The cost of the Act was to be paid out of rates and duties or of money to be borrowed (although encouraging borrowing was surely a risky path to follow).

But the Bill did not become law (the original canal company was asked to raise £10,000 for repairs and maintenance and did not), and so the responsibility for the finances of the canal remained in the hands of the Barons of the Exchequer and the management in the hands of the Caledonian Canal commissioners. An important proviso of the arrangement continued to be that an annual statement was to be delivered to the Court of Exchequer. This may seem to be a most obvious duty of any company in this parlous position, but, as the canal moved into yet another phase of operation, there seems to have been little improvement in the management structure. The administration, according to Samuel Smith, Secretary to the Crinan Canal Company from 1834, in his 1839 evidence to the select committee inquiry, fell to the commissioners of the Caledonian Canal 'by the neglect of the Government, or the Barons of the Exchequer, to issue any further directions' after the £19,400 grant was made. Telford was in charge of administration for some time, then it fell to the Caledonian Canal's legal man in Edinburgh, James Hope – and William Thomson, resident engineer, who would be closely questioned in later years for apparently failing to provide audited accounts.

From the outset, Thomson had seemed to be the very man for the job – enthusiastic and brimming with ideas. On 17 August 1819, he signed off on a document that he called part report and part prospectus, written at the Crinan Canal office, which promised improved trade on the canal and included a 25 per cent increase in the return from boat fares. This plan proposed to establish communication between 'the different parts of Lochfine [sic] and Clyde on a permanent footing', and to extend communication already enjoyed between the eastern districts of Argyllshire and the western parts of the county and to Inverness-shire. The new network of roads throughout the Highlands, Thomson explained, had shown what a difference such communication could make to individuals and communities, leading to people considering themselves 'as forming one great family, enjoying a comfort and security formerly unknown, and adding strength to the Empire'.

The numerous sea lochs and the Crinan Canal combined

with 'the late invention and rapid improvement of Steam Boats' could make Argyllshire one big happy family, too. Thomson advocated bigger and better steamboats to facilitate travel on the Clyde estuary to Loch Fyne and beyond through the Crinan Canal. This was no pipe dream. The *Dumbarton Castle* had sailed from Glasgow to Inveraray in 1815, and by the 1820s the Castle Steam Packet Company and other new shipping enterprises were creating commuter services to the villages on Argyll's sea lochs. New piers were built, and in 1839 the firm Thomson and McConnell would introduce what was known as a 'swift steamer' from Glasgow to Ardrishaig, with a connection through the Crinan Canal to Inverness and to island destinations. This was 1819 and William Thomson was showing vision.

Just as the 1792 prospectus had claimed potential profitability, so did Thomson. He foresaw a twice-weekly boat between Glasgow and Fort William, and he wanted to form a company of subscribers amongst the proprietors and others in the county and 'those connected with it', none of whom would be entitled to hold more than two £50 shares. Fares would be regulated by a committee manager at Ardrishaig, as 'the most centrical part of the passage'. Fares were to be 'moderate'. He estimated that two superior-class paddle steamers would cost £7,000. Part of his plan was to have one boat stationed at the west end of the Crinan Canal, with a 'passage boat' on the canal to convey passengers from one boat to the other, although he felt a better plan would be to have a specially constructed boat able to pass through the Crinan Canal, going once a week direct from Glasgow to Fort William and once 'to take passengers from the Lochfine [*sic*] boat, on her arrival at Ardrishaig, to Fort William'. This would save expense, passenger delays and so on.

He clearly understood that these steamboats were getting bigger by the year and that the number of passengers they carried would therefore prove burdensome in transfer along the canal. He had a range of options lined up but foresaw that an extra boat stationed on Loch Fyne would be the most economical for this potential company. In an era that had not yet grasped the potential of tourism in Scotland (the evidence of the Wordsworths and Samuel Johnson confirms this), Thomson had some excellent ideas – the mineral wells in Appin, the ruins (and in 1819 they were very much ruins) of Iona and Inverlochy Castle were just some of the suggestions he believed steamboat travel could offer access to. In time, he pointed out, the Caledonian Canal would also be on the itinerary. And, of course, access to commerce was part of his plan, too. 'What is now proposed may be the foundation of a very extensive and lucrative concern, that will stimulate and diffuse a spirit for business, for which this county, from situation, and the Caledonian and Crinan Canals, enjoys superior advantages,' he wrote. And all this would be possible for eight months of the year from March to October, as the Fort William boat would be laid up in the winter.

It was a good plan. The Caledonian Canal would be navigable from 1822, and presumably Thomson would have been well informed about its progress in 1819. And despite the fact that repairs were still needed and that the Crinan Canal iced up for two months every winter, revenues from the canal were actually picking up and Thomson was clearly operating on the premise that business generates business. The revenue for the Crinan Canal the year before he brought out this plan had been £1,603.5s.4d. In 1825, it was £2,142.14s.6d, but by 1832 it had dropped back to £1,603.17s.6d. These revenues, of course, couldn't even look at the debts owed, and it would have been a godsend had an Act in 1828 wiped out those debts. That wasn't to be, but Thomson's plan was sound, and in fact it became the way that the route operated.

However, there were those who suggested that Mr Thomson perhaps spent more time thinking of exciting tourism schemes and running his sheep farm than he did looking after the canal. At what was possibly the most comprehensive inquiry ever into the viability of the Crinan Canal, held in 1839, it was suggested that for 22 of the 25 years Mr Thomson had been effectually in charge of the canal, no audited accounts had been submitted to the Barons of the Exchequer. There were, to say the least, searching questions asked on a huge range of issues when the select committee was appointed 'to consider and report to The House [of Commons] what steps it is advisable to take with respect to the present state of the Caledonian Canal and . . . the Crinan Canal'.

The remit could be translated into modern parlance as follows: 'Is anyone taking this canal seriously? Is anyone making checks on its progress or its finances?' The canal was still under the management of the Caledonian Canal Company and, until the mid-1820s, Thomas Telford certainly had his work cut out elsewhere. But with the kind of heavy indebtedness the Crinan Canal had experienced, and the technical problems that had beset it, some stricter line of management than that experienced in the early days was obviously required for this project, so often referred to as being of 'national importance'.

William Thomson was grilled with a degree of ferocity during the 1839 inquiry, and seems to have been given little support by his colleagues. Samuel Smith told the parliamentary select committee inquiry that no checks existed on the management and that 'Mr Neill Malcolm, who resides near the canal, has frequently spoken to me about Mr Thomson's management, and the absence of any check on him.' James Walker, sent in 1838 to inspect the canal, was much more generous – he told the inquiry that Mr Thomson was 'a very active, very clever man', but that he needed an active superintendent under him to 'expedite the passage along the canal'.

Mr Malcolm (a descendent of the first Neill Malcolm to have taken out shares in the canal and the Member of Parliament who had argued for the 1828 Bill that was aimed at putting the canal back in the proprietors' hands) was himself examined on 28 June 1839 and told the select committee that he had inherited shares but that 'unless I am much mistaken no dividend was ever drawn'. He explained that although the canal was open, it had never appeared to be very efficient, but stressed its importance 'because it opens communication with the Caledonian Canal' and explained that there was now 'a considerable trade from the quarries of Easdale; the slate quarries'. These were the quarries that would be known as 'roofing the world' because their slates were exported to so many countries. In the 1830s, they were being shipped through the Crinan Canal, despite it never having been completed 'in the manner originally contemplated', Mr Malcolm noted.

Mr Thomson, he said, was one of his tenants, who had a sheep farm 'of some extent' on the banks of the canal. Asked if this was a farm 'which would divert his attention from other occupations that he might have to follow', Malcolm replied: 'It is a sheep farm, which would not take so much time as an arable farm, nor is it one of very large extent, but I believe it is conducted by himself . . . it must of course take up a certain part of his time'. The canal management was not 'vigilant' in its superintendence of the engineer, he added. The engineer's 'other occupations' were to collect the canal dues and to spend them as required to maintain the canal. Neill Malcolm was asked if the resident engineer 'gave as much of his time as he ought to do to the superintendence of the canal', to which somewhat loaded question Mr Malcolm gave the gentlemanly response, 'That I am not prepared to answer.' What he was prepared to say was that he had contracts with Thomson to supply timber to the canal. He was also willing to testify that property in a 50-mile vicinity had increased in value since the building of the canal, and he added, 'If that avenue towards Inverness were closed, it would make a considerable difference' to that positive outcome. The commissioners asked him, 'As an highland proprietor, is it your opinion that this is a work of local or of national importance?' His reply was definitive. 'I believe it to be both.'

So there were positive things to be said, but in the decade since the original proprietors had taken back management of the canal, good stewardship was in question. The blame for that seemed to fall on William Thomson, who insisted that he did indeed submit quarterly accounts but that no, he did not verify accounts under oath. His duty was to report to the commissioners of the Caledonian Canal and he had continued to do that through Mr Hope in Edinburgh. As for his sheep farm and timber contracts, he said he had permission to 'do other things' from his current manager and prior to that from Mr Telford himself. He refuted the suggestion that his sheep farm interfered with his canal work. 'I do not conceive that that occupies my time,' he told his inquisitors.

If Thomson left the inquiry that June day thinking that he had satisfied the Commission, he was sorely mistaken. A few days later he was called back because the auditor of the exchequer had told the commissioners there had never been 'any audit whatever of the accounts'. Thomson could only suggest this was a mistake. 'I know I sent the account ... with my vouchers [receipts].'

This didn't satisfy. He was told again that it did not appear that the accounts of the Crinan Canal had been audited 'in any public department'. However, James Hope, the company's law agent in Edinburgh, was another who spoke up on Thomson's behalf to the commissioners on 13 July 1839. He said Thomson submitted 'quality accounts' and that in June 1831 an audit had been carried out by the Barons of the Exchequer in Scotland. This was of accounts from January 1817 to December 1825, prior to the advance of £19,400. 'No further audit was asked for,' Mr Hope told the Commission, but added that he had done an 'arithmetical check' on Thomson's accounts – and he had asked for a check on management.

In fact, there should have been a public apology to William Thomson, because his accounts, shown in appendices of the select committee report, were very full and very detailed – and he proved beyond a shadow of a doubt that he had not been required to submit audited accounts to the Barons of the Exchequer. Thomson was sent home to Scotland to think about his evidence (and as we can imagine from televised modern select committee interrogations, it must have been intimidating, to say the least, to appear before this group of eminent committee members and have random questions thrown at him without time to prepare and with all his own evidence almost 500 miles away). With access to that evidence, he did what most of us would have done – sent off copies of the whole lot with a letter that exonerated himself.

On 9 July 1839, he wrote to Mr Hope, telling him what had happened at the select committee. He had clearly got a good system in place because he was able to lay his hands on all the required documents. He wrote:

On reference to documents here, and communications from you, it appears that, in November 1823, audits of accounts from opening the canal in November 1817, to 30th June 1823, were made. That in March 1826, audits of accounts connected with the grant of £19,400 for the great repair of 1817, appear to have been made; and again in February 1832, audits of current accounts down to 30th September 1830, appear to have taken place, all of which I consider to have been Exchequer audits; but since then no audits have come under my notice.

He asked James Hope for any clarification that he thought might help him write back to the select committee, telling him that while he was attending the committee:

a letter was received by the Honourable Chairman from the Exchequer, stating that no audits of accounts for the Crinan Canal had ever been submitted to the Exchequer, in which communication I stated there must be some mistake, for that a Treasury order existed placing the management of the canal under the Commissioners for the Caledonian Canal, and placing the money transactions under the direction of the Barons of the Exchequer for Scotland, to whom reference have been made in communications from you to this, in this I beg you to correct and explain as you see need.

James Hope replied on 13 July. He told Thomson:

. . . the only audit and settlement made by the Barons of the Exchequer of the accounts of the Commissioners of the Caledonian Canal, in regard to the Crinan Canal, took place on the 29th June 1831, when there was passed by the Barons the proper accounts of the Commissioners from the 13th January 1817, to 31st December 1825, being those relative to the application of the sum of £19,400, which had been placed at their disposal under the Act 56 Geo.3, c135, for the purpose of improving the canal.

No audit actually took place and the Barons had not subsequently called for continuation for the accounts. Had the audit taken place, Hope assured Thomson, he would have told him so: 'I shall explain to the Chairman of the Committee, that the delay of such an audit was neither imputable to the Commissioners, nor to you, and certainly was no fault of yours; your accounts having been always regularly transmitted to me.'

This was another default situation. The Caledonian Canal commissioners had let James Hope deal with the Crinan Canal accounts, not seeming to bother to check them. Samuel Smith (who had become Crinan Canal Company secretary in 1834) found papers that suggested the Caledonian Canal commissioners had really washed their hands of Crinan when the Bill went before parliament in 1828 to transfer the Crinan Canal back to the original proprietors. As for the Barons of Exchequer in Scotland, they looked on their role, according to Smith, as administrators of a mortgage. If the Treasury had wanted to sell the Crinan Canal to get its money back (although who was going to buy it?), there were differences in English and Scottish law. Samuel Smith told the 1839 select committee that he saw no advantage to be had from the Treasury foreclosing on the outstanding debts. There had been three attempts to sell the canal back to the original proprietors at the peppercorn price of £10,000, but that £10,000 would have done nothing to put the canal in proper order and pay its debts.

Asked for a summary of work that should be prioritised in 1839, the parliamentary select committee was told that there should be an extension of the pier at Ardrishaig, which had been built by Messrs Gibb & Son of Aberdeen in 1835 to facilitate steam packets and fishing boats; a lighthouse at Ardrishaig; repairs of lock gates at Crinan and Dunardry; a protecting pier at the west end of the canal; and a new section of road at Crinan. It was also suggested that a diving bell to facilitate underwater repairs should be bought at a cost of £500. This would all amount in round figures to £9,000.

Trade had increased over the previous 15 years, but the average income from the canal had for the previous three or four years been between £200 and £300. This put it on an equal footing with the Caledonian Canal, but James Walker (a civil engineer and close associate of Telford) told the select committee, 'the Crinan Canal does not appear to have been treated as if it were a favourite concern'. It still needed deeper locks and better lights for night-time safety. The reservoirs were now better able to supply the canal with water safely but general maintenance was an ongoing problem – the difficulties faced in all Cinderella situations. It is difficult to understand why the Barons of the Exchequer made just one audit and never asked for another. But if it was 'not a favourite concern', perhaps it slipped everyone's mind.

And yet, as Thomson was able to show, by 1827 nearly 14,000 passengers a year were going through the canal, and by the end of 1838 there were 59 vessels a month passing through, despite damage caused by a slate-loaded vessel that was driven by high winds against the masonry of Oakfield bridge.

The somewhat naive questions asked in the 1839 inquiry

did reveal that the world of Westminster was a very different place from Argyll. What about decent hotels? How could a vessel be allowed through the canal at nine o'clock at night in the summer months? There seemed to be little understanding of the vagaries of weather and tides, or even that several hours more of daylight are available in Argyll in summer and several less in winter than are experienced in the south of England (and this, of course, prior to daylight saving, not introduced until 1916).

In 1835, the canal had closed from 4 May to 13 July for repairs by Messrs John Gibb & Son of Aberdeen. The company had to return to fix damage to Locks 10 and 11, damaged by 'an unprecedented heavy fall of rain' that flooded the banks and locks at Dunardry and broke down the newly formed part of the bank and a cast-iron tunnel between the two locks. Such was, and is, the way the weather treats Argyll, and having to pay Gibb £2,600 for all the work necessary throughout 1835 was no mismanagement on the part of poor old William Thomson, as his meticulous accounts show. There were very naturally ups and downs. Revenues were down in 1838 because frost closed the canal for two months in the early part of the year — but the enlargement of the main reservoir meant there were no closures in the dry season because of lack of water.

There is, of course, no sign of a public apology to Thomson for accusing him of bad accounting practices. But there is a letter which must have made the select committee blush at least a little for not waiting for all the evidence before they started casting aspersions. Mr Thomson has to be admired for his record keeping. His office must have been very full and very impressive because when he went scuttling back to Scotland in July 1839, determined to show he was not the incompetent he had been accused of being in the House of Commons, he found a letter from the commissioners of the Caledonian Canal, dated 29 June 1820, which stated: '. . . you are hereby directed to pay over the balances in your hands, quarterly, to James Hope, esq., W.S. law agent to the Commissioners at Edinburgh, retaining in your hands (at the end of every quarter) £100, to meet current expenses'. In another justifying document from his extensive files, he produced a letter dated 19 July in which Mr Rickman told him: 'You need not continue to send monthly reports to the Barons of Exchequer; Mr Hope will do what is requisite at Edinburgh.'

Thomson goes on to tell the select committee in the letter he wrote with such evident relief from the Crinan Canal office in Ardrishaig on 6 August 1839: 'Having acted uniformly on these instructions, without the necessity of reference to them for about 20 years, and not prepared for examination on this or any point in particular, accounts for my not being able to state verbally in London what is now done better from this.'

He then chanced his arm – this was, after all, a select committee appointed to 'consider and report to the House what steps it was advisable to take with respect to the present state of . . . the Crinan Canal'. It had been sitting since 5 February and would wind up on 27 August. Thomson had time to say his piece. He told them, with the old verve shown in that insightful document about steamships and tourism in and around Argyll, 'I doubt not you are aware of a general desire for, and prevalence of opinion favourable to an enlargement of the Crinan Canal, on the grounds of its being necessary to obtain the full benefit of the Caledonian Canal, the trade of which, in steam-boats, with the Clyde, must ever remain cramped by the present inadequate dimensions of the Crinan.' He advised a survey, estimate and report to be prepared by James Walker to present a comparison between what had to be spent on current repairs and what it would cost to enlarge and improve.

These continuing inquiries that at regular intervals in the canal's history occupied the time of the great and the good in the privileged surroundings of parliament overshadow the lives of those people such as the Brodies who actually made the canal work on a daily basis. Of course the inquiries had to take place: so much public money had washed through the canal's nine-mile course, with often too little to show for it. But if we forget the audits that were or were not done, we can look more closely at this snapshot from 1829, which perhaps shows what life was like for the people whose livelihoods depended on it.

The annual salaries for nine lock keepers, including George Brodie at Dunardry, amounted to £22.1s.8d. The two carpenters' wages came to £7.7s.4d. There were six to ten labourers employed, eight or nine on a permanent basis. Their pay in total came to £25.4s.8d. John Cowan was paid £2.9s for breaking ice on the canal. The molecatcher who plied his skills on the canal banks (a very necessary job, considering the fragility of the banks) received £2.2s for his labour. It cost £2.6s to supply lanterns on the canal so that boats could go through after dusk. There were two smiths who worked for the canal – John Rankin in Lochgilphead and Hugh McVean at Bellanoch. John Drummond provided window glass for the canal houses and lock keepers' lanterns. The services they provided meant they were able to support their families. When the canal was closed – as it was from 10 August to 8 September 1829, because of a dry season with 'a scarcity of water' – it must have spelled disaster for some precarious household budgets.

As trade began to look up in the late 1830s, the workers may have been able to sleep more easily in their cottages at night.

What was the state of the Crinan Canal in 1839?

Good enough to keep a molecatcher in a job, but could have been better.

11

Not quite full steam ahead

The 1839 select committee never did call in any of those who worked as carpenters or lock keepers, or even those who sailed through in their fishing boats or vessels laden with slates from Easdale. William Thomson was about as lowly as the members were prepared to go, and it seemed they didn't feel they could trust him entirely without the backing of an Edinburgh lawyer's word. They did, however, seem to think the opinion of Sir Donald Campbell was worth listening to. He was a resident proprietor – important because so many proprietors were not resident and had scant real knowledge of Mid Argyll. He was also a valuable witness because he was a canal user. He had passed through many times in pleasure boats and steamers and knew the layout of the canal and the procedures. He, like Mr Malcolm, believed the canal was of 'the greatest possible utility' and had greatly increased the value of property. Close the canal, he said, and the value of property would fall 'to the great injury of the surrounding country'.

There was no denying that it wasn't in the best repair. It had, said Sir Donald, 'an air of dilapidation'. Neglect of painting and oiling and pitching of the various component parts of the canal were clearly seen by all who passed through, but he was not prepared to say if this was due to lack of money or poor management. He thought that by cutting away some 'awkward rocks' at the western end (*Oh, John Paterson, why didn't you take notice of Thomas Telford almost 30 years earlier?*) and removing mud banks at either end of the canal would cost little and make a big difference, cutting the time of journeys through the canal by two-thirds. It seemed that the workaday people using the canal were happy enough with the passage and the help provided by the canal team, but don't think that the concept of TripAdvisor is a twenty-first-century one. Sir Donald had read in a Glasgow newspaper in 1838 complaints from passengers about steamer delays. Masters and proprietors of vessels complained about access to the canal, but not the passage through it. And, of course, access was tide-dependent. Sir Donald had been detained for five or six hours because the water wasn't high enough to enter the canal and he agreed with the committee chairman, Robert Steuart, that if the mud bank was removed, most vessels could pass more readily.

In 1839, it was taking about four hours for a steamer to get through the canal and coasting vessels took longer. Sir Donald explained that a heavy vessel would be drawn by one horse and would therefore go through 'very slowly'. Steamers from Glasgow, which didn't draw much water, would have been able to enter the canal at all times of tide if the mud bank was removed, and the only other difficulty was the bends in the canal. There was perhaps a gentlemanly chortle when Mr Steuart asked Sir Donald, 'Would the bends of the canal be more likely to injure the vessel than the vessels to injure the canal?' Sir Donald agreed the vessels were more in danger than the canal – but while there was no reason not to open the canal to steamboats if masters were willing to take the risk, doing so wasn't going to increase traffic, nor was opening the canal at night going to boost trade. And although masters of vessels complained about the canal dues being too high, Sir Donald doubted whether lowering dues would increase trade.

The grand ambitions to be a canal for international trade continued to be a pipe dream, never quite coming to fruition, and as the steamers able to forge through the open seas got bigger, this was less and less likely to happen. Trade, therefore, at the end of the 1830s, was confined to coasting vessels, herring fishers and colliers. What – or who – in Sir Donald's opinion, would improve the canal? 'If government claims, and the claims of the old company, were given up, I think it probable something might be done, not as a profitable speculation, but I can conceive that the proprietors in that country would subscribe, without looking at it as a matter of speculation whether it would answer or not; I think a considerable sum might be raised if those claims were given up.'

This, of course, was the old, old story. As was the suggestion that the Tarbert route would be preferable (we know that Watt and Rennie rejected that shorter route on technical grounds, but Sir Donald Campbell said that the proprietor was 'understood to be very much opposed to it') and steamboats could negotiate better the West Loch. Sir Donald felt spending money on the Crinan Canal was the better option. Even so, these steamboats were a fly in the ointment – yes, 20 hours could be saved by going through the canal rather than round the Mull of Kintyre, but the canal vessels were 'miserably small'. Even so, James Walker, Telford's associate, told the parliamentary committee that the Caledonian Canal, much vaunted as the superior canal, wasn't in any better condition in 1839 and that the Crinan was 'capable of taking vessels of as large a tonnage as the Caledonian Canal'. If, however, both canals were in good working order (and Walker believed that £200,000 wasn't an unrealistic figure to make the Crinan workable), the route from Glasgow to Inverness could be done in two days – a day faster than could be done in July 1839.

This would be dependent on staying overnight at Corpach and at Ardrishaig, and Walker told his examiners, 'I think good inns, particularly one at the east end of the Crinan Canal, would be a great advantage.' The parliamentary committee (never quite as polite with poor William Thomson as with the likes of Sir Donald Campbell and Neill Malcolm) cross-examined resident engineer Thomson about want of accommodation in inns.

Had he never heard complaint about this lack? Well, yes, of course he had. And had it never occurred to him that the ten acres owned by the commissioners at Crinan, on which a lock keeper kept a cow and grew vegetables, could be used to build an inn? Well, yes, it had, but the commissioners 'declined going into it further than to let a portion of a house belonging to them at Crinan, which could be spared'. Inns did not seem high on the commissioners' list of priorities. This had been in the early 1820s and Thomson had to agree that the numbers passing through the canal had 'very much increased within the last 12 years'. He said there was no point in raising the matter again because the commissioners had been against it before and circumstances had not changed, other than the increase in passengers, who 'do not stop at Crinan so much now as formerly'.

This may have been a chicken and egg situation – people didn't stop at Crinan because there was no inn, and there was no point in building an inn if people didn't stop there. They did stop at Ardrishaig and usually, twice a month, had to stay on board the steamboat because the times and tides did not allow onwards passage. There was an inn at Ardrishaig, as the elevations of the early plans clearly show, but to be honest it perhaps was not the kind of inn that the late 1830s steamboat passenger wished to frequent – although when James Walker had inspected the canal in 1838, he remembered Thomson had entertained him and his colleague Mr Gibb 'very hospitably' at an inn in there. He feared that his fellow passengers weren't so lucky because there wasn't a 'suitable inn to receive them'. Thomson told the 1839 parliamentary committee that during the summer, 'when the number of passengers is very great, the discomfort is considerable'. There was a lodging house, which Thomson said was 'very comfortable' and several smaller lodging houses. Pressed on whether the inn itself was comfortable, Thomson declared it was. 'Some persons may complain of it, as they may complain of the best inns at times, but it is a fair country inn,' he told the committee. He had to admit, however, that it wasn't really sufficient for the growing needs of passengers and he was aware that there were proprietors in the area who were anxious that a good inn be built.

Mr Malcolm was one of those proprietors and he had applied to the canal commissioners for land on which to build one. He had been turned down because, according to Thomson, the commissioners 'thought it necessary to keep it [the land] in their own hands for whatever might be required and to accommodate their own officers. The application had been made directly to the commissioners, but still the parliamentary committee went after Thomson like a dog with a bone. 'Where was the difficulty in consenting to Mr Malcolm's request?' they asked. 'I have had no difficulty,'

Thomson replied. 'I had no interest in the matter; I could only report circumstances, and was bound to do so faithfully . . . but from a recent application to Mr Hope for a portion of canal ground at Ardrishaig, and his answer, I apprehend legal obstacles exist to the disposal of canal property.' This was surely the common-sense answer and the select committee should have understood that if the canal was up to its lock gates in debt and its ownership was vague, selling off a parcel of land could have led to litigation. Of course it would have been advantageous to have a good inn built at Ardrishaig (although Thomson couldn't remember there ever having been mention of an inn when the question of the land was mooted). Was it part of Thomson's job description as canal engineer and superintendent to sell off parcels of land on which to build inns? Thomson felt he had done his duty by telling the commissioners about the request. If he saw something relating to improvement that he thought advisable, of course he would recommend it. Badgered on an issue that seems beyond his remit, he could only agree, when the question was put every which way, that of course better accommodation would be of benefit to the canal and yes, he would look on such plans favourably.

Able to gather his thoughts once he had returned to Scotland, Thomson said in his much more confident letter to the select committee that money should be spent on a decent road to facilitate transfer of passengers along the canal, and pointed out that 'The state of the canal funds have hitherto not been such as would warrant an outlay to build or increase the accommodation of the inns at Crinan.' While it might have been possible to add this to Mr Walker's estimate for improvements, Thomson's shrewd suggestion was to build another lock keeper's house, freeing up the present lock keeper's accommodation to be added to the inns already existing at Crinan, and then encourage the neighbouring proprietor to provide public accommodation – two 'respectable' smaller places being preferable to one larger establishment as they would increase competition, split the outlay and produce a suitable return. The two inns at Crinan were run by Margaret Kerr and Margaret McLachlan, and they were perhaps of the same quality as the one in Ardrishaig, where Walker and Gibb has been entertained well – but as the world became more sophisticated and people expected better (and quicker) service in all areas of their lives, this little canal was going to have to offer more.

James Walker had commented in a letter written to F.T. Baring (Secretary to the Treasury) at Great George Street, Edinburgh, on 7 June 1838, on one of the suggested ways to speed up the transfer of passengers from the Glasgow-Ardrishaig steamer to the Crinan-Inverness boat – the building of a railway on the canal banks. The letter appeared in an appendix to the parliamentary committee the following year and reads:

> . . . by this (even if worked by horses) passengers might be conveyed in an hour with greater certainty than they are now in four. A steamer of proper dimensions for passengers would work from Glasgow, etc., to Ardrishaig, and from Crinan to Inverness. For cheap passengers and heavy goods, the present steam-boat going less frequently than at present would suffice. That this would increase the despatch and character, and therefore the extent of communication, cannot be doubted; but the increase must be great to warrant such an establishment of steam-packets, which would of course be a private concern.

Walker had said he didn't think the cost of laying a railway on the banks would be heavy, but he was clearly more keen to see money spent on repairs and upgrading, including the clearing of the mud from each entrance and the removal of as much rock as possible to widen the canal.

This would not have been a steam railway. Although prototype steam-powered rail transport had been invented in 1804 and Robert Stephenson designed his 'Rocket' in 1829, railways were still isolated private ventures and it would not be until the new decade opened that the railway boom would begin.

From 1 April to 30 June 1839, 1,378 passengers travelled through the canal. It was the slates, fish, timber, eggs and coal that brought in the modest revenue collected by John McDougall at the Ardrishaig end and John McIntyre at Crinan. It was clear from the line of questioning at the parliamentary committee inquiry in 1839 that creating a better environment for passengers – better inns, faster links, better service – was the way to go.

Their recommendations, given on 21 August 1839, were somewhat more negative than this suggests. The committee saw no prospect of the government obtaining any return of their advances. There were no grounds to expect an increase in traffic under the current management or that the income would increase to meet the improvements needed for it to move into the black from its exceedingly red position. They advised, therefore, that an Act (yes, another one) should be passed foreclosing the mortgage and putting the canal in the hands of the treasury to take 'such steps for the future support and management of the Canal as they may deem advisable'. The message to private enterprise was to put up – or the Treasury would have to shut up and dispose of the property.

Only bleak comfort could be taken from the fact that the Caledonian Canal owed over £1 million and there were harsh words about its premature opening in 1822 that had led to 'numerous accidents', failures of certain sections and 'the source of continual expense'. So – even Big Brother seemed doomed. And yet a new decade would bring something of a miracle turnaround. One has to suspect that John, 7th Duke of Argyll, descendant of one of the main instigators of the original Crinan Canal plan, was its main engineer.

12

Famine, feast and flower girls

There had been a national financial emergency during the building of the Crinan Canal. In 1797, the government had to suspend cash payments so that London bankers and their clients could maintain their credit. In 1816, when loans were being sought to keep it open, a gold standard had to be introduced by the Bank of England to regulate the economy. Government projects such as the roads, canals and harbours to be built by Telford were part of a government recovery scheme to get out of the additional financial mess created by the recent wars. In 1825, when the canal was undergoing yet another of its many economic predicaments, Great Britain endured what has been called the first modern financial crisis, when neither war nor some cranky investment scheme could be blamed – the fault lay in the main with the branching out of the finance economy into tiny investment units. The economic problems created by the 1825 crisis had a terrible knock-on effect on ordinary people. Alexander Dick, tenured assistant professor in the Department of English at the University of British Columbia, suggests that it is 'little wonder' that 'many novels by Dickens, Trollope, Eliot and Hardy are about financial catastrophes and economic calamities' experienced as the century progressed.

There was quite a strong Scottish influence in attempts to reform the economics of the day, with J.R. McCulloch's voice crying loudest to establish an effective gold standard against which paper money would be regulated, and a curb on extending credit to landowners. A series of articles in the *Edinburgh Review* and *The Scotsman* were convincing but far from popular with those, such as Sir Walter Scott, receiving the extended credit.

In the mid-1830s, there were poor wheat harvests and Great Britain had to import too much of its food to be healthy for the Bank of England's monetary reserves. Small banks still had a licence to print money – their own bank notes – which led to inflation, as too much money flooded the economy. Lots of paper money was lent but there were no real reserves. The attempt to curb the lending was disastrous – interest rates were raised from 3 to 5 per cent and the result was a financial crisis that seeped across the Atlantic to America. In 1839, when the parliamentary committee was deciding the future of the Caledonian and Crinan canals, the country itself was just about as leaky as both waterways. The Bank of England had to borrow £2 million from France – the country with which it had so recently been at war. In 1844, the Bank Charter Act cut back on private banks being able to create paper money and eventually only the Bank of England had the power to create money in England (Scotland's banks continued to issue their own notes). But tinkering with the system and borrowing out of a crisis, many modern economists would argue, can never put anyone in a good position to deal with those bear traps that life sets in unexpected places.

People had been lulled into a false sense of security in the early 1840s, as industrialisation took hold. Stephenson had now adapted our friend James Watt's steam engine and what was officially known as 'Railway Mania' began. There were plans for railway lines throughout the country and the price of railway shares rocketed by 98.4 per cent between January 1843 and August 1845. All this was based on speculation, of course. Just like the canals, Acts of Parliament had to be passed to allow a railway to be built. By 1846, 272 such Acts had been passed. New railway companies proliferated and 9,500 miles of railway had been proposed.

Of course, it was exciting. The country must have been buzzing – already there were new roads, canals, villages and harbours, factories were springing up everywhere and manufacturing was creating a new middle class with some money in its collective pocket. Now the amazing steam train was to set sweep across the country and bring modernity and prosperity to all. With the possibility of putting down a 10 per cent deposit on shares in a railway (albeit with the railway companies allowed to demand the remainder whenever they wished), what was there to lose except the opportunity to make a fortune?

What was to lose, of course, was the railway bubble itself, which would burst because it was illusory and transient, just like the South Sea Bubble and the Darien Scheme before it. The little companies had bigger companies upon their backs to bite them into submission. Bought out, many of the little companies' big plans didn't come to fruition. Some bigger companies planned their finances badly and went out of business. And, of course, there was fraud. 'Buy our railway shares now' was often a con, and once they had parted with their money, too many investors never saw an inch of track laid. Rather than 9,500 miles of railway, around 3,000 miles were actually constructed, leaving subscribers out of pocket.

And just as it was becoming clear that this was an over-promotion of the possibilities, the Bank of England, which had reduced interest rates at the beginning of the decade, now raised them, and banks started to reinvest in bonds, diverting funds that could have been invested in the railways. As companies such as Great Western Railway began to buy up the little companies at rock-bottom prices, the members of this new middle class found themselves with empty purses. Canal mania had been followed by railway mania, and neither had made the fortune promised to their investors.

Times were hard for everyone and the potato famine didn't make them any better. Quite rightly, we associate the potato famine with Ireland because it was most devastating there. But in Scotland, the blight that had been imported from America in 1843 also had dreadful effects. Since the 1740s, the potato had ousted barley and oats as the 'fill up' food of the Highlands and Islands because it was cheap, easy to grow in poor soil and also nutritious. The damage done to the 1845 crop was restricted, but in 1846 the blight turned potatoes to stinking pulp and there was real famine. People had to scavenge for what food they could find and as they grew weaker they were more susceptible to disease. There were outbreaks of dysentery, scurvy and cholera that proved fatal for many.

In Ireland, landlords and the government itself had refused to assist the victims of the famine, with catastrophic effect. In the Highlands and Islands of Scotland, many proprietors did help (although those who didn't were remembered for generations). The Free Church organised distribution of meal and transport to the Lowlands, where 3,000 Highlanders found jobs building railways. The army and navy also distributed rations, which were fixed at a pound and a half of meal per day for a man, three-quarters of a pound for a woman and half a pound for a child. This help came to an end when the worst of the famine seemed over, but although it looked as if the potato crop would succeed in 1846, wet weather created ideal conditions for the blight to strike again, and again in 1848.

Measures to help the starving, including government-paid labour, involved building walls and digging ditches, and constructing roads and piers. Named 'destitution roads', some gave access to areas of Scotland that had previously been unreachable. Even so, a third of the Highland population emigrated. The government couldn't keep up with the need for relief and the burden fell on the landowners again. The Duke of Argyll offered special terms to his tenants to migrate to Canada under Relief of Destitution measures in 1847, following the suggestion of a paper written by the Revd John Duncan Lang that £1 or £1.10s be available to each adult emigrant on landing in Canada, 'for which the Poor Law Union or the promotion of any well-organised emigration usually provides'. Lord Murray wrote to the Marquis of Lorne on 7 February 1847, 'I shall rejoice to find things take a better turn', adding that emigration was 'indispensible [*sic*] for the welfare of the Highlands'. That year 1,059 people emigrated from the Duke of Argyll's estates alone.

In a lengthy letter written to his cousin, the Marquis of Lorne, on 13 January 1847, John Francis Campbell of Islay (known as Iain Og or 'young Iain') suggested that the expansion of the Crinan Canal could be 'a boon to our unfortunate district'. Campbell enclosed a copy of a letter he had written to the 'Governor of Southern Australia', Sir George Grey, seeking advice on behalf of 'a great number of Highland gentlemen' whose tenants were in desperate straits. The advice that came back suggested that Australia didn't offer a favourable climate for the Highland and Island folk, and that emigration to Canada would suit them better. However, Campbell was really seeking to improve the lives of those who remained in the country. He reminded his cousin, 'you yourself are aware that the Tyree [sic] men were so unhappy in Ayrshire that they preferred returning to starve at home rather than undergo the misery of never understanding or being understood by those around them'. The Tiree men would, of course, have been Gaelic speakers, like the majority in the Highlands and Islands. Instead of trying to find them work in an alien environment, Campbell suggested that 'the Home Office or the Treasury would have the rough plan and estimate for the enlargement of the Crinan Canal', which he had seen as long ago as 1830. He wrote:

> A Government Engineer could easily examine these plans, and verify them with very little trouble if the Government chose (as I boldly say they ought) to give this boon to our unfortunate district, and thus enable our wretched fellow creatures to earn sufficient wages to support both themselves and their families.

Campbell had worked out the maths. In 'ordinary years', a Highland family could be supported on £2 per head – the cost of three bolls of potatoes at eight shillings a boll (a measure equating to 140 lb) and one boll of meal. He reckoned that at the current prices, inflated by the crises, 'it will cost £5.12s 6d per head to keep him alive for a year'. He explained that the ordinary wages in the Highlands and Islands were £15.13s a year. This would obviously feed 'a man with a wife and four children', and at £2 a head there would be money over for other essentials. At current prices, 'for a man to feed, or rather to keep this family alive, it will cost £33.12s. Supposing that this year his wages be doubled and that he receive two shillings in lieu of one shilling he can only receive £31.6s to pay for the food, which will cost £33.12s.' This was a man who understood fully the needs of the 'ordinary' man. Wages for making drains (a major government scheme at the time for which landlords were being given government grants and which would cost the government £458,523.9s.1d in Scotland) 'must always be on a low scale', he pointed out, so these would be truly 'destitution ditches'. Campbell felt the drainage scheme (although in the long term a beneficial one) would leave men unable to support their families. He was also fearful for people's sensitivities. 'There is many a true hearted Highlander . . . who would scorn to receive alms like a pauper.' Although the Free Church's aid scheme was 'meritorious', he thought 'unless this fund be distributed with the greatest delicacy and judgement, it will ruin the people, and crush proper pride of the proprietors'.

The expansion of the canal would have been an excellent means of helping families to survive this disaster, and the people of Mid Argyll were Gaelic speakers, able to make island migrants welcome (better a Gaelic dialect than an incomprehensible Scots tongue). But later in January 1847 more than 100 heads of families in Tiree had given their names for emigration, even as the drainage work went ahead. Tobermory was designated as a harbour for emigration from the Western Isles; some were offered a free passage to Australia, and Mr Mclean, the Tiree minister, wrote to the Marquis of Lorne in deep distress about the 'fearful crisis' that was 'accelerated and dreadfully aggravated by the failure of the Potatoe [*sic*]

Crops'. The rise in population had exacerbated this crisis and the general cry was that the government should intervene to stop a 'vast deal of destitution and misery'.

A big problem was that the Colonial Land and Emigration Office at Westminster was not best pleased with the idea of Scotland's working men pitching up in Prince Edward Island. In 1841, Canada had officially become a province and Charlottetown on Prince Edward Island was the setting of the new Province House. The Marquis of Lorne was told in no uncertain terms in March 1847 that 'it would be quite a mistake to send mere labourers' and that land was only available for 'small farmers possessed of some little means'. The families signing up to emigrate to Canada couldn't scrape a bowl of porridge together, let alone pay for land on the other side of the Atlantic. William Cunard, son of Samuel Cunard, who in 1838 had founded a shipping company, told the Marquis of Lorne that capital of £50 to £500 was needed to set up a life in Canada. An annual wage in 'good' years of just over £15, which was now stretched to unattainable limits by doubled food prices, was hardly going to yield savings to buy into this dream. And yet they went in their thousands and some from Crinan Harbour itself.

Government officials were loath to see the administration of the Poor Law mixed up with new relief committees. Objections were raised in the House of Commons and in February 1847 any plans of meeting the distress in Scotland through grants of public money were off the agenda.

It was perhaps the frustration of being unable to alleviate this sorry situation that led to plans being hatched for Queen Victoria to visit Argyll and travel through the Crinan Canal. To have that royal seal of approval would surely have an effect on the canal's revenue and, through that, on the livelihoods of the men who had work in any way connected with it.

From John, 5th Duke of Argyll, to the latest inheritor of the title, George, 8th Duke (Marquis of Lorne until the death of John, 7th Duke, on 25 April 1847), the heads of the Clan Campbell had been the major players in the progress of the Crinan Canal. Despite the shifting sands of ownership and management of the canal, there is no doubt that this family maintained very close supervision. In troubled times, as we have seen, it was to Inveraray (latterly, as we have seen, to the Marquis of Lorne, as the old duke's health weakened) that people appealed for guidance. Floating the idea of enlarging the canal to provide work would have been seen as placing it in influential hands, if addressed to the Marquis of Lorne, now the Duke. With the death of his father, this Liberal politician became Master of the Household of Scotland (a major role in the royal household) and Sheriff of Argyllshire. Access to Queen Victoria was obviously his 'job', as Master of the Household of Scotland, but he was also a close associate of Prince Albert. He had married 'dear Lady Elizabeth Leveson Gower', as Queen Victoria referred to her in her *Highland Journals* (her full title was Lady Elizabeth Georgina Sutherland-Leveson-Gower, daughter of the 2nd Duke of Sutherland and Mistress of the Robes to the Queen – she had met her future husband in 1842 when she accompanied Victoria to Taymouth Castle), and this made royal connections still more closely knit.

Victoria and Albert had married in 1840 and they had made their first visit to Scotland in 1842. They were most impressed by the scenery and this was to be the first of a number of visits until they leased Balmoral in 1848 before buying it in 1852. An invitation to visit this couple that they both knew so well in a Highland setting would, therefore, have been accepted with alacrity and pleasure – but one does have to wonder if the new duke was not just a scientist and politician but a good public-relations man as well. Yes, with the work that had been done to repair and upgrade the canal since the 1840 Parliamentary Report this had become a recognised route to the Highlands. But with his tenants at death's door and digging ditches to keep their families out of the poor house, if sending Victoria and Albert along the canal was the duke's doing, it was either crass insensitivity or a stroke of genius.

The outcome of the Queen's voyage (or rather, voyages, because she made the return trip) shows the itinerary to have been the mark of pure brilliance.

The royal couple left Dartmouth on 12 August 1847 and sailed north to reach the Clyde on the 17th. At Greenock, there were crowds lining the quaysides, but also 39 steamers 'over-filled with people', as the Queen reported in her diary, followed the royal vessel. On Wednesday, 17 August, they sailed almost to the very door of the 'new' Inveraray castle (it had been built between 1745 and 1760 during the construction of Inveraray, as Scotland's first planned town) and were met at the pier by the duke and duchess, and the duchess's mother and sister, with Campbell of Islay (so concerned about the welfare of the people) among those in the welcoming party. Pipers led the royal carriage to the house, where the queen had her first meeting with her future son-in-law, the then two-year-old Marquis of Lorne, who would grow up to marry Princess Louise. She described him then as 'a dear, white, fat, fair little fellow with reddish hair, but very delicate features, like both his father and mother'. Princess Louise would be born the following March.

They lunched with the Argylls, then boarded *The Fairy* and made back down Loch Fyne, arriving at Lochgilphead – 'a small village where there were numbers of people, and, amongst others, Sir John P. Orde, who lent his carriage and was extremely civil' – at five o'clock in the afternoon. Victoria, Albert, the royal children and 'our people' drove to the canal, 'where we entered a most magnificently decorated barge, drawn by three horses, ridden by postilions in scarlet'. We joke about today's royal family thinking that everywhere smells of fresh paint: perhaps Victoria and Albert were under the impression that three horses, garlands of flowers and scarlet-jacketed postilions were everyday accoutrements for the average fishing boat and steamer passenger heading for Oban.

If the garlands and postilions impressed Victoria, the journey itself didn't. She succinctly summed up in her journal entry for that day what people had been saying for decades – and what had been emphasised ad nauseam at that 1839 parliamentary inquiry. Yes, it was smooth, and, yes, the scenery was 'very fine'. However, she added:

> . . . the eleven locks we had to go through – (a very curious process, first passing several by rising, and then others by going down) – were tedious, and instead of the passage lasting one hour and a half, it lasted upwards of two hours and a half, therefore it was nearly eight o'clock before we reached Loch Crinan.

To be fair, the time may have been dragged out by the singing and dancing children who saw the royal couple off from the east end of the canal. Be that as it may, despite hurrying onto the *Victoria and Albert*, which lay in wait for them at

Crinan, it was too late to go on to Oban and their journey was lengthened by a day. However, as she wrote — and no doubt discussed with her friends, and the word must have got around — having spent the night at Crinan, she found it 'a very fine spot, hills all around, and, in the distance, those of the island of Jura . . . the blaze of numerous bonfires — the half moon, the stars, and the extreme stillness of the night — had a charming effect'.

The fulsome praise for the rest of the journey, which led them to Oban — 'one of the finest spots we have seen', where the population was already heading up to 2,000 — Mull, Iona, Staffa and the then tiny Fort William. They left their yacht there and travelled by carriage to stay in a hunting lodge owned by Lord Abercorn. Albert went on to Inverness and then saw the Caledonian Canal, which he told Victoria was 'a most remarkable work', before they returned south to Crinan, where they were received by 'Mr Malcolm, whose castle is just opposite' and entered the canal at 10 a.m. Although 'the people kept running along as before, and there was a piper at each lock', they reached Lochgilphead in pouring rain by noon and sailed on the *Black Eagle* south to Campbeltown to meet the royal yacht again.

Half a century previously, the whole concept of the Crinan Canal had been to avoid the dangers of the Mull of Kintyre. Now the *Victoria and Albert* sailed round it, so that Queen Victoria and Prince Albert could take the scenic route along the Crinan Canal.

By 1846, there had been 36,000 passengers travelling through the canal (perhaps not quite so impressive as the 30 million who had travelled by rail in 1845) and the patronage so publicly bestowed on it by those royal journeys made in August 1847 would have a marked effect on its fortunes.

Victoria and Albert's journeys may have been smooth (if tedious) but that was not to say that all was now perfect for the canal. It was just much better than it had been for most of its existence. Cinderella had gone to the ball – and while she wasn't quite freed from the kitchen, the future was looking brighter.

13

Towards the Linnet *years*

In the years between the weighty parliamentary inquiry into the status and viability of the Crinan Canal in 1839 and Victoria and Albert's visit in 1847, there had been the usual attempts to repair, maintain and improve – always hampered by weather and the canal's basic construction. William Thomson was still the resident engineer and his official annual report for December 1846 was forwarded to the Lord Advocate of Scotland in early 1847. This was, of course, when the whole of Great Britain was suffering financially, and in the Highlands and Islands of Scotland this was exacerbated by the start of the famine. Around 200,000 people were affected, and by the time Thomson was writing this report, the Free Church was beginning its aid programme, providing rations regardless of denomination. The engineer was clearly affected by these circumstances. Having carried out some pitching work to the south side-face of the canal summit, Thomson reported that the work was almost complete 'so as to admit of reducing in January [1847] the number of labourers employed (no very agreeable duty under the present circumstances of the country) retaining the most necessitous to complete the operation'. Campbell of Islay was hoping that men could be given the job of enlarging the canal to alleviate the increasing poverty — but that was clearly at best a distant possibility, and at worst nothing more than a pipe dream. And here was Thomson distressed at having to lay off men because a job was done and he had no excuse to keep them on. It was almost a certainty that they would now have to receive handouts from the Free Church aid programme.

Although Thomson reported that the weather was dry, there had also been 'some days of severe frost through December'. It is hard to imagine the plight of those men as they walked away from the canal, their bellies empty, their pockets empty, and the ground as hard as iron. Did they have to go and join the 20 folk already on the local 'poor roll'? The frost had been severe enough to interrupt navigation through the canal, but it was kept open with the help of 'trackage', or horse-drawn trackboats, and indeed more canal steamers passed through in November and December 1846 than had for some time. December had seen 147 boats and vessels going through, paying dues of £186.4s.2½d. There was some comfort in the fact that two carpenters were kept in a job carrying out repairs to ice fenders, as well as mending lock gates and wheelbarrows, but of course, whatever work was done increased expenditure, which for the last quarter of the year was over £374.

Earlier in the year there had been storms that damaged the Glen Clachaig reservoir. Extra work was done on the Lochanadd Tunnel to safeguard against the kind of disasters experienced in the past. The water shortage of 1845 had through these measures been averted in 1846, despite increased traffic. Thomson foresaw that in 1847, with work done on bridges and lock gates in 1846, he would be able to concentrate on protecting the canal bank-facings. There is clearly no hint that the canal would experience a royal visit in the summer of '47, and if there had been, when Thomson was writing the report he could have seen no cause for celebration, as he performed the painful task of laying men off.

A new wharf below Lock 5 at Cairnbaan had been completed in May 1846. Thomson reported that if this had been in use for the whole year, 'it would have saved 114 lock fulls of water, as many openings and shuttings of the bridge across Lock No 5, and consequent interference with the thoroughfare of the public road', not to mention lengthier journeys for the vessels themselves. The improvement, Thomson explained, meant 'the avoidance of 1,026 partial interruptions to tracking and to the passage of vessels out and into this lock'. He was optimistic that if revenue continued to be as good throughout 1847 as it had been in 1846 (which had actually covered the cost of the work on the reservoirs), work on necessary dredging could be carried out. There was never a report in which leaks were not mentioned, and one that was wasting too much water had been in existence at the second basin at Ardrishaig. A road between Crinan basin and the Parliamentary Road at Kilmahumaig was needed 'to give the public safe access by conveyances with the steamers calling at Crinan'. These were all on Thomson's shopping list for 1847, along with the run-of-the-mill repairs and maintenance that could always be expected. The steam packet owners had communicated to Thomson that they wanted better facilities at Ardrishaig for the 'increased traffic and enlarged description of steamers in Lochfyne [*sic*]', along with a supply of pure spring water and gas lamps at the locks and wharfs at Ardrishaig. The water and lights were, Thomson thought, within budget; the bigger and better accommodation was not. There had been 37,000 passages through the canal in 1846 and Thomson said that if this was to increase, more gas lamps would indeed be a good investment, as it would keep 'a good order on the pier by the exclusion of carts and horses at particular times'.

Claims had been made against the canal management because of holes dug to provide spoil for repairs of banking, and a boundary fence had been called for. There seemed to be a common conception that the Canal Act had lapsed and local landowners were trying to muscle in on any revenue the canal was raising. Thomson advised his management to seek legislation to prevent a door being opened not only to fleece the canal of its revenue but also to create 'indefinite and continuous interruptions to the tracking and trade of the canal'.

There had been requests for dues to be reduced. Thomson saw this as placing the canal management between a rock and a hard place. If the dues were reduced, the revenue would go up because traffic would increase. But increased traffic would create more damage and a need for more reservoirs. However, Thomson had the welfare of the people at heart in the dire circumstances that the current crisis had imposed. He wrote:

> the Reporter takes the liberty of recommending the early and favourable consideration of this measure [reduction of dues] to the Commissioners, by which the inhabitants and coasting trade of almost the entire Western coast and Islands of Scotland, especially to the West of the canal, may be expected to derive a degree of benefits and with the reasonable expectation of rather improving than injuring the canal revenue.

The expenditure during 1846 had included the salaries of the engineer, harbour master, lock keepers and bridge keepers, a sum of £552.17s.4d. Day labour for general repairs and unexpected incidents had cost £956.5s.2½d. Extraordinary outlay – including work on lock gates, embankments, pitching, the wharf at Cairnbaan and the replacement of 40-year-old equipment – came to £2,449.17s.9½d. Revenues had amounted to £2,526.6s.1½d, compared with around £1,372 in 1822, £1,900 in 1834 and £1,950 in 1840. The number of passengers who had gone through the canal by boats in 1846 was 13,345, and by canal steamers, 4,192 – a grand total of 17,537 – while 573 boats had used the canal and 1,449 vessels.

Remembering that a main selling point in the late eighteenth century had been that the canal would aid fishing boats, confronted as they were then by the dangerous Mull of Kintyre route, Thomson's figures for 1846 are particularly thought-provoking. In 1818, dues from fishing trades had been £418.10s.10d. Now, in 1846, the figure was £165.9s.9d. The figures for coal cargoes were almost reversed – in 1818 they had accounted for £149.7s.5½d, while in 1846 the revenue was £441.11s. In 1846, slates and coals topped the list of cargoes going through the canal. Cattle, sheep and lambs had also increased in numbers since the early days. Barrels and boxes of herrings shipped had risen from 1,851 in 1841 to 3,439 in 1846.

In 1843, a wharf and slip had been constructed at Crinan to accommodate the passenger steamboats. Steamer dues had been dropped from 2d to 1d on 1 August 1844, and now steamer companies were proliferating – Lochfyne Steamers and North Line Steamers were two that paid their dues to use the canal.

Thomson's report of 1846, seen by the Lord Advocate, must have seemed more positive than any submitted previously. The powers-that-be may, therefore, have been well disposed to read his June 1847 report that suggested the canal management was on better footing. A suggestion was made that the original company of shareholders might be induced again to take up their cudgels – but, as had been the case when such suggestions were floated in the past, the government expected the old company to come up with some reasonable sum that indicated they were willing and able to maintain the canal. In 1847, neither the government nor the original shareholders were in any position to put cash on the table, but a revision of the system was expected.

After all his trials and tribulations, it is good to know that William Thomson at least was still in post when Victoria and Albert sailed through 'his' canal. He was replaced in the autumn of 1847, having given the best years of his life to a project that could never have given him (or anyone else connected with the canal in a managerial role) real job satisfaction. It is doubtful if any commemoration of over 30 years in service was given, but he could have felt some gratification to know that in his first report in 1848, Charles Herbert, the new resident engineer, gave a list of repairs to be done – but said that generally things were 'in good order'.

His quarterly reports over the decades provide fascinating, if often depressing, evidence of the progress of the Crinan Canal. So much more business-like, objective and professional than those of his predecessor John Paterson, they are a true resource for engineers and historians alike. When he was asked by the Reverend Alexander Mackenzie, minster of South Knapdale parish, to assist him by providing a report for inclusion in his contribution to the 1845 *Second Statistical*

Account of Argyllshire, Thomson delivered a summary of that first half century of the canal very clearly and precisely. Knowing, as we do, that he was able to put his hand on letters and reports from the earliest years with the ease and alacrity we expect from modern technology, the contribution he made to the *Statistical Account* must have pleased its editors immensely.

And then, by yet another Act of Parliament, passed on 14 August 1848, the Crinan Canal was 'vested in the corporate body entitled the Commissioners of the Caledonian Canal'. In other words, it was back in the hands of Big Brother. The commissioners were made a corporate body and while the revenues were assigned to the Exchequer, the Caledonian Canal commissioners were to oversee spending. They didn't even bother to articulate the interest that was due on the public debt on the canal (which in itself was £74,400). During the debate leading to the passing of the Act, it was said, 'it is just and reasonable that the said canal and works connected therewith should be held at the Disposal of the Commissioners of Her Majesty's Treasury, freed and discharged from all the Right, Title, Interest, Claim, and Equity of the said Company of Proprietors, or of any Person or Persons claiming from or through them'. It was seen to be 'essential that the Crinan Canal and Works Connected therewith should be vested in the Commissioners of the Caledonian Canal, in order that both Navigations may be united under the same management'.

The Act named the new commissioners: there was to be nothing left to chance. The world had become more proficient at running enterprises and keeping hold of the purse strings. The Speaker of the House, the Chancellor, the Lord High Admiral, the Vice President of the Board of Trade, a member of the Treasury (at the time, William Gibson Craig), a clutch of MPs, including 'Duncan Macneill' (*sic*) as MP for Argyllshire, and then his successor, Neill Malcolm, Alexander Campbell, Edward Ellice Junior, James Murray Grant of Glenmoriston and Evan Baillie, 'and such other persons as shall or may be appointed as herein after mentioned'. The tolls and rates accrued from the Crinan Canal and its properties would become the property of the commissioners. 'If the Commissions shall within 20 years of the passing of the Act pay or cease to be paid £74,000 plus interest and also all such sums of money as the Commission shall have expended', then all the canal and its properties would revert back to the Company of Proprietors.

Just when things seemed to be going well, with the royal visit successfully over, business beginning to pick up and fewer major construction problems to be faced, responsibility was taken away. Of course, most of those who had dreamed the dream of this waterway to connect with everywhere from the islands to the Baltic, and of the prosperity it would engender, were long gone. Their heirs had, in the main, given up on ever seeing a penny's profit for their ancestors' investments. The Crinan Canal was now 'an asset' to be subsumed into other organisations, privatised or nationalised, as was seen fit by its financial masters of the day. Even Neill Malcolm was on the list of new commissioners because of his public persona rather than because Neill Malcolm I had invested personally in the original ideal of a canal to make profit and serve the people.

Nevertheless, the canal really did begin to blossom. Whether it was the royal visit (the canal was now known as the Royal Route) or the shrewdness of the new Caledonian Canal commissioners, business was good. Since the provision of improved landing facilities at Ardrishaig, two steamers a day called in there in winter and two or three in summer. Some of the passengers were heading for Oban and Inverness. Others came to Ardrishaig and stayed there, putting money into local enterprises and helping the whole Loch Gilp area to develop. William Thomson put the development of Ardrishaig and Lochgilphead down to 'the fostering care of John McNeill, late of Oakfield, with his late father (whose property these villages were)'. But, of course, had there been no canal, there would have been nothing to foster and, in reality, McNeill had demanded a ridiculous sum in compensation for the lands to be used for the canal (beaten down to sense, or the canal budget would have been squandered before a pick entered the clay). By 1854, the canal was carrying 35,000 passengers, 27,000 sheep and 2,000 cattle. This was double the 1846 passenger figure of 17,537. The figures for sheep and cattle reflect not just an upturn in the Crinan Canal's revenue, but the major changes that were happening throughout the Highlands – changes that prefaced still more hard times for the 'ordinary' people, who would be pushed off their crofts in favour of the far more profitable sheep, and in turn by the change in the landscape to grouse moors and deerstalking, which were also to prove more lucrative for landowners than producing crops and grazing cattle.

Black cattle had had their day. They had been the mainstay of the Highland and Island economies for centuries, coming by drove roads and across dangerous stretches of water to the major market in Kilmichael Glassary just north of the canal. There they had been sold on to markets in Falkirk and, after changes in the law, across the border to England. Now their price couldn't match what landowners could expect for sheep meat and wool. And, of course, sheep didn't need so many people looking after them. Vast acres could be turned over to raising them, while the crofters were moved out. More package deals were to be offered for emigration, although the history of the Clearances suggests less favourable options were open to thousands. However, the passengers, sheep and cattle were helping the Crinan Canal and its environs to flourish. Charles Herbert was surely having an easier life of it compared with his predecessors.

But no. The heroine of this story is the Crinan Canal and she is more often a tragic heroine than one who gladdens her audience's heart. In 1859, a reservoir dam burst. Millions of gallons of water, along with hundreds of tons of rocks, boulders, peat and mud were released, spreading in both directions along the canal and wrecking locks, pounds, a public road and canal banks. No one was killed, but the devastation was catastrophic.

A lengthy report in the *Illustrated London News* and an article in *The Spectator* of 1 January 1859 revealed the seriousness of the situation.

The bursting of the reservoir embankment was caused by the 'tempestuous' weather of January and February 1859. A letter to *The Times*, which was then printed in the *Spectator*'s 'Scotland' news round-up on 12 February 1859, described the situation graphically:

After an unprecedented wet season, on the evening of the 2nd, about eight o'clock, one of those reservoirs, becoming overcharged, suddenly burst and precipitated itself into the one beneath, which also giving way, the contents of both bounded into a third, and, with a roar which shook the country for miles round, an avalanche of water, rocks, and earth rolled down the mountainside, furrowing a deep watercourse in its way, and instantly obliterating the canal under a mountain of thousands of tons of rocks and stones. The vast body of water, separating into two great tide waves, rolled away to the east and west, breaking up lock gates like tinder; and, tunnelling vast chasms through the banks, the waters found vent over the open country, the one by the town of Lochgilphead into Loch Fyne, the other over the Crinan mosses into the western sea, both strewing the face of the country with mud, stones, peat, fragments of corn-stacks, uprooted bushes, and broken timber, in a most wonderful manner. Even the loch for many miles out to sea is quite turbid, and its surface speckled over with floating debris.

Though the loss of property is at present incalculable, yet, most miraculously, there has not been a single life lost, though the alarm of the people of Lochgilphead may be conceived when they heard the distant bellowing of the torrent and rolling and grating of rocks, and then saw through the darkness of the night the moving flood all around them.

About half a mile of canal is buried under a chaotic heap of Cyclopian stones, like a rugged sea beach. In this part of Glen Crinan Nature has completely resumed her sway – towpath and high road, and all appearance of the hand of man, have totally disappeared.

For two miles the canal is destroyed, the banks being cut up by chasms like railway cuttings; but the remaining portions, about four miles at either end, are intact, though probably injured by the quantity of mud injected into them. The pressure upon their banks must have been great, as the waters swelled over their edges for their whole length, and Ardrishaig was probably only saved by the immediate opening of the sluices and giving vent to the water, which must, had the bank given way, have swept the village into the sea.

The dramatic effect on people as far away as Lochgilphead is vividly captured in these words and, although the phrase was not in use until the 1920s, newspapers were learning that 'a picture paints a thousand words'. On 5 March, the *Illustrated London News* proved the point by publishing an image of the scene looking east from Dunardry. The Dunardry locks are damaged beyond recognition, and the roadway is badly cracked to the east of the cottages on the canal bank, while to the west of them the road simply becomes a jagged gaping maw such as we would see after a bomb blast or an earthquake. In a brief verbal reminder of the January story, the paper talked of 'an avalanche of water, rocks and earth rolling down the mountainside, furrowing a deep watercourse in its way, and completely obliterating the canal under a mountain of thousands of tons of rocks and stones'. Referring to the image, the report added, 'The two boatsheds for the trackboats are shown crushed and useless.'

George May, engineer from the Caledonian Canal, was sent to survey the devastation and by August of that year the matter had reached parliament. A Motion was made on 4 August to the Committee of Supply, which was discussing a range of civil service estimates. Based on George May's survey, the committee discussed:

That a sum, not exceeding £12,000, be granted to Her Majesty, for the purpose of restoring, in the year ending the 31st day of March, 1860, the Crinan Canal, which was destroyed by the failure of one of the Embankments, caused by the tempestuous weather in January and February, 1859.

There was a somewhat fractious debate, with Colonel Fitzstephen French, MP for County Roscommon, saying that not only did a good many people 'not know what or where the Crinan Canal was', but that having been a 'private speculation of the Campbell family', it had cost the public purse a considerable amount, 'had never yielded anything back to the Exchequer', and now that a further £12,000 was required, 'would it not be better to hand it over to private parties?' He added the broadside, 'if they can get anybody to take it'. Fellow MP W. Williams thought it was high time to take a stand against grants to repair the canal, which together with the Caledonian Canal had 'cost this country £1,400,000'. Mr Williams saw the Caledonian Canal as 'a still greater failure than the Crinan' and quoted abysmally low revenue for the previous year. It was pointed out, however, that it had been an 'extraordinary flood' that did the damage to the canal. The previous Conservative government (the Liberals under Viscount Palmerston had come into office in June 1859) had allocated the £12,000 for this 'urgently needed repair' and it had been suggested that the canal should be increased in size and adapted for large ships at a cost of £80,000, but this had been a step too far and the Conservatives had not sanctioned so great a sum from the public purse.

The Committee had just discussed cleaning the waters of the Thames, for which London was to be charged a rate. It was suggested that if the Crinan Canal were to be repaired, a rate could be charged to Scotland. But there were those MPs who just didn't see the point of the debate – the undertaking was 'a losing one' and 'the public as a whole derived no benefit' from it. The Chancellor of the Exchequer, however, was quite clear on the point of the vote. It was 'for the purpose of repairing the effect of a sudden accident'. Was the House going to allow the traffic of the canal to be stopped, and the canal itself to go to ruin, for want of timely reparation? That, the Rt Hon. William Gladstone told the Committee, would be irrational. The late government would have been inexcusable if they had not ordered the repairs. It was true they had done so without the authority of the House, and very properly, that had to now be rectified. Unfortunately, those who opposed the grant of £12,000 had been given ammunition by George May, who had written in his report, 'It has been impossible to trace the failure to any more immediate cause than the original imperfection of the embankment.' Those against were, therefore, able to score points with the line 'The money now asked for might be as well thrown into the canal at once.'

The debate fell into the old argument (still raging to this day) about the support Scotland received from the population of England, but it was pointed out that the canal was not the property of Scotland but the whole nation, and that as a public work it would be foolish to 'let it go to rack and ruin for want of the necessary repairs'. And several members of the Committee pointed out that the £12,000 would restore the reservoir and the canal, which was 'a great convenience for a large district of Scotland'. It could be an even greater convenience if it were enlarged for large steamers. Patrick Smollett, who had succeeded his brother Alexander as MP for Dunbartonshire in June 1859, spoke in favour of the grant and urged fellow Scots MPs to do the same. When the Committee divided, the Ayes had a majority of 47 and the vote was agreed to.

Repairs went ahead, but in June of 1860 the Caledonian and Crinan canals were back on the parliamentary agenda, with the same old arguments about their costs, the drain on the public purse and their low revenues. This time a Caledonian and Crinan Canal Bill proposed to raise £20,000 more from the Loan Commission. MPs fumed that this was 'a perfect waste of public money', reminding the House that 'some years ago, after it had cost £1,300,000, it had been offered as a gift to any one who would take it, and no person was found to avail himself of that offer'. It had been made the subject of no fewer than 17 Acts of Parliament, and one MP regarded the whole proceedings connected with its construction or its repair 'as the grossest job' that had in his time been perpetrated. If the Loan Commissioners granted this money, 'they might as well throw it away'. The Crinan Canal was too small, while the Caledonian Canal had been built at a time when it was thought it would be useful in a war situation. One MP said the canals had never been of any use to anyone, while another argued that 'the maintenance of the canal was of national interest and importance'. The Prime Minister himself, Viscount Palmerston, spoke in favour of the Bill, if only because it protected the public purse.

On 23 July 1860, the Caledonian and Crinan Canals Amendment Act was passed, enabling the commissioners to improve both canals, to buy land and construct necessary buildings. The commissioners were to be allowed to license or grant permission to establish 'manufactory, distillery or other works', using the water for such works and the sides of the canals. The Caledonian and Crinan canals were leased to private undertakings in 1860. After such a disaster as was experienced in 1859, and the delays caused by the lengthy debates in parliament about whether the canal should or should not be given enough money to repair it, it was nothing short of miraculous that in 1866 the commissioners had ordered a specially designed steamer to work on the canal. But then, it was already a miracle that the canal was still open, still operating, and now experiencing an ever-growing traffic in passengers, livestock and freight.

14

The Royal Route takes off

The parliamentary prejudice against ensuring that two Scottish canals were maintained could have had an adverse effect on the fortunes of the Argyll waterway. Celebrity, however, was a force to be reckoned with even in the mid-nineteenth century, and whatever the authorities felt about maintaining a loss-making canal, the public couldn't get enough of it. The so-called Royal Route was becoming the fashionable destination of the growing middle class. From the 1850s, the population of Great Britain began to grow at a rate that would have concerned Thomas Malthus far more than the eighteenth-century statistics that led to his prediction that food supplies would not meet the demands of the expanding populace. It increased from 20 million to 36 million between 1850 and 1873. During the whole of the nineteenth century, Scotland's population grew from 1.6 million to 4.5 million, and between 1851 and 1871 it rose from just under 3 million to 3.25 million. At the same time, wages went up by around 80 per cent and life expectancy began to increase as health conditions improved. There were changes in what people did for a living. By 1861, 19 per cent worked in agriculture, 39 per cent in manufacturing and 27 per cent in services.

Modern economists are fairly gloomy about Britain's progress during these years (mainly because other countries, in particular America, were doing a bit better). But there was a real increase in the number of people who were being paid enough to have cash to spend on items other than essentials. Some of that was spent on travelling – day trips and short holidays. They may not have been able to fully emulate the gentry who made the Grand Tour around Europe in the eighteenth century, but they were determined to see as much as they could of their own country and others. Since the beginning of the nineteenth century, the middle classes had become 'tourists', and the combination of steamboats, the railway, and more disposable income meant that tourism was an industry that was taking off. Some areas were, of course, off limits – the French kept on having revolutions, and that deterred all but the bravest, especially in a year such as 1848 when cannons and heads rolled at regular intervals. Staying on home territory seemed like a good idea, especially as the British rail system (despite becoming shaky as an investment) was superior to the French one. Scotland was unique in having such a quantity of beautiful and imposing scenery to be seen from the deck of a steamboat.

Those who chose the Royal Route – Glasgow to the Crinan Canal, then on to Oban, Fort William, and the Caledonian Canal to Inverness – travelled through the canal from Ardrishaig with the help of horse-drawn track boats. Victoria and Albert had sailed on the *Sunbeam*, so it must have been a thrill in itself for those passengers who could say they had trodden the same deck as royalty. The other track boat was *Maid of Perth*. Passengers travelled to Ardrishaig on the *Iona* or the *Chevalier*, both owned by David Hutcheson & Co., the company that had been established in 1851 with three partners, David and Alexander Hutcheson and David MacBrayne. David Hutcheson had been a manager with J. & G. Burns, which ran a steamer service to the Inner and Outer Hebrides. Hutcheson's new company took over these routes and began to make money on the profitable Glasgow to Ardrishaig mail run, as well as transporting passengers and freight to the outer western islands.

The enterprise that really took off, however, was the summer tourist run to the western isles. The new 'tourist class' not only put money in the Hutcheson coffers but also helped to develop the villages throughout the Islands, and improve the economy of remote communities in a way that the original canal investors could never have envisaged. The Duke of Argyll had thought his tenants would have been able to find better markets for their produce, that his quarries and other enterprises would benefit from access to the Central Belt economy and that the fishermen would be better off not having to go round the Mull of Kintyre. The idea of 'ordinary' people paying to jump on a boat and traipse round the islands for pleasure was as alien in 1793 as cheap sunshine holidays were to the pioneers of aviation in the early twentieth century.

The company contracted J. & G. Thomson Ltd to build their steamers. By 1864, it was the third *Iona* that was in service. The first had been sold to the Confederate States in America but had sunk on its way through the Clyde estuary. The second had no better luck, but the third became much loved by the new tourist class, along with the *Chevalier* and the *Gondolier*, both launched in 1866. These were the seagoing vessels. The company also asked J. & G. Thomson to build a small screw steamer, the *Linnet*, which would replace the horse-drawn track boats taking passengers between Ardrishaig and Crinan. The public really fell in love with this steamer. The *Linnet* had two screws and was 34 tons in weight, 86 feet long and 16 feet broad, with a shallow draft of 2.8 feet. That meant she was well suited to go through the canal locks, and her blunt canoe-shaped bow was designed so that she could push into the opening canal lock gates. She sailed down the Clyde on her maiden voyage on Friday, 1 June 1866, and the following Monday, the *Glasgow Herald* reported:

> A small saloon steamer, named *Linnet*, proceeded down the river on Saturday to take her station on the Crinan Canal in connection with the Royal Route to the Highlands. Her construction is quite unique, and we doubt not but she will prove a valuable adjunct to the comfort of the numerous tourists while on their way through the Highlands.

She did indeed 'prove a valuable adjunct'. Ardrishaig became a busy village (so busy that by 1867 a public toilet had to be erected), and while their luggage went ahead on carts, the passengers were free to walk along the towpath. Once aboard the *Linnet*, it went slowly enough for them to get on and off at the locks, and the shop at Cairnbaan became a top favourite. Local people were quick to take advantage of their visitors. Musicians and dancers would watch for the *Linnet* at the locks, where the passengers had little to do but wait while the boat was ushered through by the lock keepers. While the water levels changed, they would perform Scottish dances and play the pipes, and the visitors obliged by lobbing coins for them onto the towpath and wharfs. The *Linnet*'s summer service lasted right through until 1929.

Not all passengers went on to Oban and the north. Some took a carriage and explored locally. From 1801, John

MacNeill of Gigha had begun to develop properties from his Oakfield home around Loch Gilp. From Kilmory, at the other end of the loch, a small village was laid out around the quay at Paterson Street. By the 1820s, there were industries in Lochgilphead – a dye works and water-powered mills (too late for the 525 people who had sailed on just one day from Crinan to North America in 1819 because there was not enough employment for them at home). The Orde family (later the Campbell-Ordes) altered Kilmory Castle with the help of Joseph Gordon Davis, the renowned Scottish architect. Botanist Sir William Hooker was called in to design the gardens. MacNeill was, of course, 'old money' and his comparatively modest house at Oakfield reflected that, while Kilmory Castle was a showy 'new money' place revealing the ostentation of the new industrialists' lifestyles.

Oakfield was sold to the guardians of a young army careerist, Alexander Campbell. They had bought it when he was 21 and he was impressed enough to give up the army to become a farmer, restoring the estate's Gaelic name of Auchendarroch and bringing his bride, Harriet Keir, there to live in 1841. The couple drove across the canal bridge to be welcomed by what Harriet called 'a world of people' employed there. Having found that little had been done by this army of servants, the next morning the new Mrs Campbell sent a number of them packing, leaving only a 'good cook, a kitchen girl, my maid, one housemaid, one laundress, one butler and a boy, and a groom and a boy' (from Harriet Campbell's *Memoirs*, transcribed by Alan Campbell and quoted in the 90th issue of *Kist*, the magazine of the Natural History & Antiquarian Society of Mid-Argyll).

The existence of such establishments in the corridor of the canal suggests that farming could be successful, but often money was made elsewhere – the Malcolms had many business interests at home and abroad, and although their lands had been developed well (James Gow's drainage being a case in point), the funding for the new Poltalloch mansion that was built in the 1840s did not come solely from rural activities but from enterprises embedded in the growing industrialised society to the south.

Despite the burgeoning tourist trade, which included day-trippers, artists, ornithologists and budding historians, there was always that 'Mr Micawber' feel to the canal's finances: in 1864, income was £3,602 while expenditure was £4,545. Even as the tourist trail expanded, the dues paid were never enough to make money for the canal, however successful the enterprise made Messrs Hutcheson and MacBrayne. But there was a period of half a century from 1866 to July 1916 when the commissioners could say in their 111th report that the Crinan Canal Company had worked 'without any loss' and with no government subsidy. That must have given the successors of the original company some small sense of satisfaction, even if the remaining surplus of £7.5s.7d would scarcely pay for the management to have a day out on a steamer from Ardrishaig to Glasgow.

The *Linnet* was clearly a key factor in the success of the tourist side of the canal's operation, and if the fishing fleets diminished, there was an increase in the transport of cargo through the canal on Clyde puffers – the little cargo vessels that were specially designed to fit the dimensions of the Forth & Clyde and Crinan canals. The puffers delivered coal to the west coast, bringing back whisky and other produce, including slates and kelp, and all the other items that back at the beginning of the adventure the proprietors intended as the main freight that would be carried through the canal.

There had been a huge slate trade in the first half of the nineteenth century, when seven quarries employed around 500 men in the so-called 'slate islands' off Easdale, on the coast north from Crinan towards Oban. That came to a halt when a terrible storm in 1850 flooded the excavations. With no pumps to get rid of the water, the industry that had been able to boast that it 'roofed the world' dwindled. Slate from Ballachulish, however, continued to travel south to Glasgow and Edinburgh via the Crinan Canal.

Barley was a cargo that came to the canal and stayed there. There had been a distillery in Ardrishaig since 1815. By 1828, five years after the Excise Act began to put whisky production on a legal footing, it was producing some 76,000 gallons of whisky. The Glendarroch Distillery, owned by Henry Hoey & Co., moved to the banks of the canal in 1831. It was founded at the Glenfyne Distillery and was sometimes referred to as the Glengilp. It was sold on in 1852 to Peter MacNee and then to William Hay & Co. in 1857. What the distillery's legal status was during those years is questionable, because under the 1860 Amendment to the Caledonian and Crinan Canals Act, the commissioners could give out licences to develop factories and distilleries on the land adjacent to the canals. Glendarroch by then was 29 years *in situ*. The distillery changed hands a number of times throughout the rest of the nineteenth century, eventually closing just before the Second World War, although the warehouses continued to operate from 1937 to 1970.

An account of a visitor to the distillery in 1887 gives a vivid picture of what the journey to the Crinan Canal had become. Alfred Barnard explained that his party had left Greenock on 26 July by the *Columba*, 'one of Mr David MacBrayne's swift passenger steamers', headed for Ardrishaig. He was obviously much taken with the *Columba*, saying, 'The boats on this route are fitted up with every imaginable convenience and contrivance for the comfort of passengers. On board there is a post office, with telegraph and money order departments, a daintily stocked fruit shop, bookstall and a magnificent dining saloon.'

The *Iona* and *Grenadier* were still running on this route in the 1880s and evidently were equally impressive. Barnard extolled the virtues of the scenery, too, and by then there were seaside resorts accessed by piers, and there were many who commuted by steamer to work in Glasgow – some daily and some staying in town all week and returning to their families and impressive new sandstone villas on Friday evenings. Alfred Barnard thought the combination of good steamers and stunning scenery were what made the Glasgow to Ardrishaig route 'one of the most popular of Mr MacBrayne's "summer tours".'

By then, of course, the inns that caused all the discussion 40 years previously had been put in place. In fact, some of the small and less salubrious places of accommodation had opened and been closed down again. However, the Royal Hotel (today the Grey Gull) was an impressive establishment by then and just a couple of minutes' walk from the canal's Lock 4. It can be assumed that is where Barnard was to stay. 'We reached Ardrishaig at 1pm and, after securing quarters at the hotel, made our way to the "Glendarroch", distant about half a mile,' he wrote. Most flattering is his mention of the canal: 'The distillery is planted on the banks of the far-famed Crinan Canal and is quite an object of curiosity to the thousands of tourists who on board the celebrated little canal steamer *Linnet* pass by on their way to Oban.'

So – 'far-famed', 'celebrated', 'thousands of tourists': the mean-spirited MPs who debated the fate of the canal after the terrible natural disaster of February 1859, saying that few people knew either what the Crinan Canal was or where it was, should have been forced to read Alfred Barnard's account and perhaps then to eat it in a bowl of cold porridge.

Describing the location of the distillery itself, Barnard talks about the Darroch River that cascaded down a 70-foot course into a trout pool before passing through a tunnel beneath the canal and on to the sea. A walk up the glen went from gardens filled with hawthorn and lilacs to heather-clad hills above. Views across the loch and over to Kilmory Castle (renovated some four decades previously) seen at sunset helped him to understand why 'this lovely wooded glen is a favourite resort of tourists and artists'. He also gives an insight into the legality of the early whisky operation, suggesting that the name 'Robbers' Glen' referred to smugglers and their stills in the hills.

The Ard burn fed the 1880s distillery, which covered three acres and had a frontage on to the canal 500 feet long. The manager, Mr Hunter, told Barnard that barley was brought to the distillery by canal, the vessels discharging their cargo at the granary doors. Water from the hill behind the distillery went into the distilling process, and the water from the loch and the Darroch burn provided the power. There was a new kiln on the site that Barnard described as 'one of the finest we have seen in this part of Scotland'. Fired with peats, it dried 1,000 bushels of malt at a time. The four warehouses, which could hold 2,000 casks of whisky, housed just part of the distillery's production – more was stored at Waterloo Street in Glasgow. This was a major operation.

Glengilp House had been the residence of the distillery owner but was now the manager's house, with a large garden full of fruit trees and flowers stretching to the canal banks.

The company's two resident excise officers, who lived in adjacent houses, shared this garden. There were also eight houses for workers, each with a small plot. To the rear of the distillery was a peat shed containing 500 tons of peat, and there was a cooperage, stables and cart sheds beside the distillery worm tub. Some 80,000 gallons of the pure Highland malt were produced by the distillery at that time, according to Barnard. He was as taken with the scenery as with the whisky, which he sampled at Glendarroch House, home of the 1887 proprietor William Gillies, who fired a signal gun to warn his guests that it was time to enjoy his hospitality. A distillery vessel was evidently at the disposal of the guests to take them to their 'quarters' and back to Glendarroch House for, one assumes, a Glendarroch dram.

Barnard wrote that the beauty of Glendarroch House was 'unequalled' in the district, 'skirting the canal for a considerable distance' and forming a 'fringe of brushwood and trees festooned with honeysuckle and other trailing plants, familiar to all who have passed along this lovely route on their way to Oban and the north'. Whether he penned this before or after the Glendarroch House hospitality, there is still a truth in the description of the banks of the canal, changed though they may be in the smaller details by the passing of 130 years.

15

Into the twentieth century and more plans for change

Had Mr Barnard travelled to the Glendarroch Distillery some eight years earlier, he might not have written quite such a glowing account of the canal. In 1880, there was a dry summer and, with no water in the reservoirs, the canal had to close for 16 weeks. Despite some bigger vessels now using the canal (the revenue for 1878 had been £6,000), there would always be the built-in problems of the Crinan Canal – that it was too small, and that there was either too little water or too much water. There had been suggestions throughout its history that it should be increased in size, and of course the first options offered by Rennie had been to either take the 'Dell' route or one across the Crinan Moss to Duntroon. The latter would have allowed for a deeper and wider channel, but Rennie opted for the 'Dell' route with its higher summit.

In 1896, when the Canal Tolls and Charges (Caledonian and Crinan Canals) Order Confirmation Act was passed, setting a new range of fees for vessels passing through the two canals, it was clear that the kind of traffic using the waterways had changed enormously in a century. The Act lists very detailed classifications of cargoes and types of vessels, and pleasure craft now featured prominently. Everything from bobbins to coffins, butter to black oil in casks, sheep dipping powder to photographic apparatus, mustard to optical instruments, white of eggs to 'hair for head dressing' were specified in the Act – alongside the more expected cargoes such as granite, manure and basic slag. Busy though all this makes the canal sound, many were not happy with its capacity. In 1892 Captain Donald Dewar, owner and master of the *Jura*, a steamship designed to sail through the canal, asked Argyll County Council to approach the government for a new ship canal. Despite the history of negative government responses to any development (or even repair) of the Crinan Canal, the council agreed in principle. In 1896, Captain Dewar had worked himself up into some real action and got 11 owners and charters of herring steamers to sign a petition to be sent to the commissioners of the Caledonian and Crinan canals, seeking pressure on the government to consider the ship canal plan, stressing its importance to the Scottish fishing industry and the national economy.

Although the authorities were not biting this bait, this was an era of proliferating engineering projects that were increasingly ambitious and imaginative (it was in the 1890s that a very serious plan for a tunnel between Antrim and Kintyre was proposed). It was only to be expected that the Crinan Canal would attract attention. Engineers would have understood that although the canal was carrying these varied cargoes, the fishing industry would be vastly improved if the canal were bigger. This was a challenge that was taken up by Crouch and Hogg, Engineers of 175 Hope Street, Glasgow, who published a memorandum on a proposed ship canal in May of 1896, rehearsing the history of the canal, stating that the natural increase of traffic from the Clyde to the West Highlands had led to the adoption of larger vessels than the Crinan Canal could accommodate, resulting in a decrease in its revenue, which would probably continue. Although around 30,000 passengers were passing through the canal each year and the income was now averaging about £5,300 per annum, the memorandum stated bluntly that 'The present Canal is not only altogether out of date, but it labours under many disadvantages which restrict its usefulness, and so prevent its Revenue from expanding with the increasing trade of the country.'

The disadvantages were listed, and by now there are no surprises: the canal could only be accessed at Ardrishaig for six hours in each tide; the small size of the locks meant the larger vessels now heading for the Western Highlands had to go round the Mull of Kintyre; passenger traffic could only be handled 'at very great inconvenience' through transfer of passengers and luggage between Crinan and Ardrishaig (the passengers went by steamer, the luggage in vans by road); the Crinan end of the canal was 'tortuous', with few passing places and many rocky corners; the height of the summit frequently led to closures in summer because of a lack of water (when the canal was closed for 16 weeks in 1880, the revenue lost was £1,500); and the canal was expensive to work and maintain because of the numerous locks. Even if the summit level was lowered some 34 feet, the 'limited size of the Locks at either end would still restrict the traffic'.

So, what to do? Crouch and Hogg wanted to build a ship canal that would start at the head of Loch Gilp, pass to the west of Lochgilphead, then follow the valley of the Badden burn to near Cairnbaan. The stretch from Cairnbaan to

Barnakill would 'practically coincide with that of the existing Canal'. It would then take off across Crinan Moss and the basin at the mouth of the River Add and terminate in Loch Crinan. This is a route that sounds rather familiar. The length of the proposed ship canal would be six miles from lock to lock and it would 'enable ships to enter at all states of the tide'. The entrance channels in Loch Gilp and Loch Crinan would be dredged to a depth of 20 feet at low water and it was proposed to make the canal 20 feet deep and 80 feet wide at the bottom, except at the entrance channels, which would be 100 feet wide at the bottom. It was conceded that the width of the water level would 'of course' vary according to the nature of the materials in the excavation. It was what they found when they started to dig the original canal that led to compromise and difficulty, and perhaps Crouch and Hogg would have encountered similar difficulties. The Glasgow engineers, probably feeling rather superior to their predecessors of 100 years ago, suggested a summit level of 12 feet above sea level and there were to be two locks side by side at each end of the ship canal 'to facilitate the working of the traffic'. These would be 350 feet long by 55 feet wide, and 220 feet long by 30 feet wide. They foresaw that 'with the exception of the rock cutting at the summit between Cairnbaan and Barnakill, and probably a little rock near Badden, the excavation throughout would be of the simplest character, and could be done by Dredgers cutting their own flotation as the work advanced'. The spoil would be used to reclaim some 300 acres of foreshore at the head of Loch Gilp. No embankments would be required.

Today, we are used to major companies offering some 'added value' concept to their proposals – the playground or new road as a bargaining tool for planning permission for a new supermarket. Crouch and Hogg suggested that their scheme would incorporate a harbour for fishing boats and a wharf for landing passengers and goods at Lochgilphead, and a wharf on the ship canal itself near Island-Add Bridge for the Bellanoch and Kilmartin districts. These proposed major changes to the Mid Argyll landscape also included road diversions. A new road would be built on the north side of the canal, meaning that traffic between Lochgilphead and the Kilmartin and Kilmichael districts 'would not have to cross the canal'. Instead, there would be swing bridges over the canal at Lochgilphead, Cairnbaan and Island-Add. One of the most exciting and innovative proposals was that electric power and lighting could be installed. The memorandum says:

> At a point about a mile to the west of Cairnbaan there is ample water power from the Knapdale Hills for the establishment of an electric installation, which would not only supply power to work the Lock Gates and Swing Bridges, but also to light up the Canal when required.

Hydropower was in its infancy. An electrical technology exhibition had been held in Munich in 1882, and the Alpine and Nordic countries began to develop the techniques they witnessed there. Sir William Armstrong had worked with Joseph Swan, inventor of the light bulb, to use hydroelectricity to power his mansion, Cragside, in Northumberland not long after the influential Munich exhibition. There were similar small-scale projects in Scotland, such as that developed by the monks in the abbey at Fort Augustus, whose small 18-kilowatt scheme was installed in 1891 to power their electric organ and the local village. The Crouch and Hogg plan to use hydroelectricity in 1896 to work the mechanics of a ship canal and the canal banks was indeed cutting-edge. Scottish engineers were in the forefront of this pioneering work; the innovative British Aluminium Company completed the Kinlochleven hydroelectric power system and aluminium smelter in 1909, just 13 years after Crouch and Hogg considered this embellishment to their ship canal scheme. The Kinlochleven plant was a world leader: Crouch and Hogg obviously were aiming to participate in this newest wave of engineering. They certainly thought big. They foresaw a drainage area for their ship canal extending 60.5 square miles and 'embracing the whole watershed of the River Add and the Kilmartin Burn, as well as the present gathering ground on the Knapdale Hills'. There was to be a dam and weir across the channel at the mouth of the River Add near Crinan, forming a large storage reservoir. The canal would become for 0.2 miles a dredged channel through the reservoir marked out by buoys.

They had not, when they presented the memorandum, carried out sufficiently detailed surveys to be able to estimate the rock excavations that would be needed, but 'allowing a liberal margin for contingencies, we think £500,000 would be an amply sufficient estimate for the work'. Once constructed, the West Highland steamers would be able to use the canal instead of going round the Mull of Kintyre, enabling a large increase in passenger and tourist traffic. The Glasgow-Oban service could be expanded, two transfers would no longer be necessary and instead of a seven-and-a-half-month gap in passenger provision each year, this would be a year-round operation. Fish steamers would save on the loss of a day's market. In 1896, there were 15 fish steamers running to Glasgow, but 12 were too large to pass through the Crinan Canal. Yachts had been getting bigger and better too, and many of them were too big for the present canal. The ship canal would accommodate them. There were still horse-drawn vessels on the canal: the ship canal would have no towpaths, but tugs would form part of the working plant of the canal and these could generate income.

With the sophistication that had come with modernity, bodies such as the Fishery Board, the Lighthouse Commissioners (the Stevenson family had been very busy up the west coast, installing lighthouses in awkward places) and the Submarine Mining Engineers would, Crouch and Hogg believed, be able to use the ship canal for their steamers and vessels. They estimated that the gross revenue would be £16,500 a year, with working expenses at £5,000, leaving a net revenue of £11,500. Interest rates at the time were 2.5 per cent and this amount, the memorandum suggested, would be enough to pay the interest on a loan of £500,000. Within a few years, increased trade would bring a 'fair return on the capital expenditure'. In the early 1790s, similar projections had been made for the Crinan Canal and subscribers had bought into it with enthusiasm. This time, no half a million was forthcoming.

However, as the century ended and a new one began, complaints about the state of the Crinan Canal didn't go away. John Groves, the canal's resident engineer since 1885, wrote a further document in 1905 about the canal's deficiencies. By this time, only three steamers trading regularly with the Highlands and Islands could actually use the waterway and the fish steamers were, so to speak, in the same boat. He produced the Crouch and Hogg plans, which by now were supported by a detailed survey. Alterations to the existing canal could be carried out for £745,000, while the new ship canal could be constructed for £796,000. There was a Royal Commission on Canals and Waterways, which sat from 1906 to1909. The Crinan Canal was not the only one to be considered, of course – the eyes of the commissioners were cast over the whole country's network. The evidence given in relation to Crinan rehearsed yet again the positives – the range of cargoes (coal, kelp, timber, granite, slates, produce and the rest), and the 30,000 passengers – and the negatives (worn out, obsolete, too narrow, too shallow, and one cutting comment, 'hardly fit to be called a canal at all'). The fact that so many people enjoyed just being there apparently was not yet a good enough reason to maintain and repair it.

It really had outlived its original purpose of aiding the fishermen: factory ships now collected fish from smaller vessels and took the catch to market in Glasgow. A gentleman named Duncan Lamont who had been involved in the fish trade for a quarter of a century said the Crinan Canal was 'of absolutely no use whatever to the fresh fish or fresh herring trade of Glasgow'. And although it enjoyed a very healthy tourist trade, even this was criticised in evidence to the Royal Commission. Captain John Williamson of Turbine Steamers Ltd, a company that had been set up in 1901 to operate TS *King Edward*, the world's first commercial turbine steamer, explained to the commissioners that if the proposed ship canal were constructed, 'a great passenger traffic would be created between the Clyde and the West Highlands'. He put a word in for the construction of the proposed ship canal, saying that 'The loss of time and the expense in getting to Crinan by the present route is strangling the great passenger traffic which should now be in existence.' Captain Williamson had, of course, a somewhat subjective viewpoint. He had gone into business with Charles Parsons and Company, a

Newcastle engineering company that was pioneering the marine turbine. Three new turbine steamers were, when he gave evidence, operating alongside Williamson's fleet of older paddle steamers and a ship canal of the dimensions that suited his new steamers would have benefitted his developing business venture.

The arguments presented by Crouch and Hogg in their original memorandum of 1896 were reiterated to the Royal Commission, and there was even a plan floated for a canal between the two Lochs Tarbert. The commissioners must have read the reports of James Watt and John Rennie from the late eighteenth century, because they countered this suggestion with the fact that on emerging from West Loch Tarbert during a south-westerly gale there could be very rough seas for up to 12 sea miles north of the island of Gigha. Tourists would be exposed to these seas, whereas the Crinan route avoided them. The supposed haven of West Loch Tarbert would always present this lurking danger. Suggestions that parallel canals at Tarbert and Crinan could accommodate all sizes of vessel were met negatively – while the Crinan may have been dilapidated, the Commission could see no justification for two canals so close together. The final report of the Royal Commission said that the evidence had not been strong enough to convince the Commission that, were money to be poured into either repair or the commissioning of a new ship canal, the return on capital outlay would be considerable enough to justify the public expense. However, public money should be considered in terms of alleviating poverty in the Western Highlands and Islands. If goods could reach these areas from the Central Belt more quickly, the costs would be less and the people would benefit. The Royal Commissioners intended well but did not leave any lasting legacy: in today's world of rapid transport systems, the people of the Western Highlands and Islands are still subject to high prices and some transport companies even refuse to deliver there.

It was the joint argument of improved fish transport and increased tourism that was convincing enough for the report to say that the case could be made to 'justify a liberal grant of public money to meet such smaller contributions or guarantees as might be obtained locally and from traders'. In other words, match funding if there were contributions from other sources. Perhaps they hadn't read any of the reports written between those of Watt and Rennie and those at the start of the twentieth century — this offer had been placed on the table time and again with no takers. What they were most seriously aware of was that any public funding would have to be voted for by parliament and they could see that a vote for money for a new ship canal might more readily gain 'Ayes' than funding to repair a 'worn out' canal 'in need of extensive repairs and alterations'.

At this distance, the commission sounds fair and relatively positive compared with some of the nit-picking and snide comments that emerged from nineteenth-century inquiries of this sort. The report concluded:

> . . . the development of local trade and local tourist traffic, Your Majesty's Government might fairly make it a condition of the grant of public money that some of the counties and the trading interests (including those of Glasgow) concerned in the future use of this route should give practical expression to their interest in its development either by local contribution or by guarantees.

Having made this suggestion to various witnesses throughout the lengthy inquiry, it had, the Commissioners said, 'not been unfavourably received'. Poor districts obviously would not be able to contribute, but arrangements might be made so that other areas and individual traders or companies could 'combine to make some offer'.

The commission reported in 1909, and in 1910 the Treasury instructed Sir John Wolfe Barry and Partners to start work on repairing the Crinan Canal so that it could 'continue to be used for its present purposes'. The £31,650 allocated for this didn't, according to the commissioners of the Caledonian and Crinan canals, allow any improvements, and those rocky corners were still causing problems. The sea lock at Ardrishaig also needed to be enlarged and there was no leeway for such improvement. The canal commissioners applied for a bigger grant in 1911 but the Treasury didn't think development was practicable, passing the buck to the Secretary of State for Scotland. The public was not satisfied. The *Glasgow Herald* reported on 27 September 1912 that the Clerk to the Argyll County Council had given notice to the Glasgow Corporation of a meeting to be held in Oban about the ship canal proposal and asking representatives to attend. It was commented that the Oban venue was short-sighted, as there would have been a greater opportunity for a successful meeting if it had been held in Glasgow. Nonetheless, on 10 October 1912, the newspaper recorded, 'A meeting of the representatives of Local Authorities and others favourable to the construction of a ship canal was held in the Argyllshire Gathering Hall, Oban, last night, MacLachlan of MacLachlan, convenor of the county of Argyll, presiding.' The meeting attracted quite a crowd – not just members attending the meetings of the council but farmers attending the autumn sales at Oban. This would not just have been an extra entertainment for the farmers – the livelihoods of many would have been affected by the efficiency or otherwise of transport.

It fell to Mr J. Patten MacDougall of Gallenach, C.B., to move what the *Glasgow Herald* called 'a lengthy resolution', the crux of which was that after 110 years without improvement, the Crinan Canal was 'insufficient for present-day requirements', that freight services were therefore very high, and that the construction of a canal 'capable of passing expeditiously the largest steamer trading to the Highlands would be of the greatest benefit to the district by cheapening and accelerating communication with the Clyde ports, and that the bringing of the entire district into closer touch with its southern markets would do much to arrest the serious depopulation now in progress'. The resolution added that the Royal Commission on Canals and Waterways had reported:

> [a] strong case has been made out for an improved communication etc., and the fact of the existing canal having been worked for the last 50 years without loss and from statistics obtained of traffic available for the proposed ship canal it is believed that the latter, in addition to being self-supporting, would give a small return on the cost of construction – in view of these facts this meeting ventures respectfully to point out to the Government that should the Crinan Canal be allowed to remain any longer more than a century out of date they will be obstructing progress and withholding from a wide and necessitous district an important aid to prosperity.

It was a good idea. And the Crinan Canal was now an old lady in need of so much care and attention that she was a burden on her nearest and dearest and on the state. There were many who spoke in favour of the proposal, including Mr W. Murray Morrison of the British Aluminium Company at Kinlochleven, who said that his company 'strongly favoured' the project. More than 60,000 tons of material was used at the company's works at Kinlochleven and Foyers, all water-borne. The newspaper reported: 'He believed that was a small proportion of what would come to the West Highlands when they were opened up by the introduction of water power . . . They were willing to co-operate in every way in promoting the scheme.' The Reverend Malcolm MacCallum, chair of the Lorn District Committee, said he believed the construction of a ship canal 'would have the effect of breaking the merciless shipping monopoly by which they were oppressed'. There was evidently applause for Mr MacCallum, and for the Duke of Argyll's chamberlain, Alfred Lewis, who believed that rates on agricultural produce would drop if a ship canal were built. He raised a laugh (though it was no doubt tinged with irony) by offering the statistic that 30 shillings a ton was the price of shipping grain from Glasgow to Bunessan, while the same item could be shipped to Singapore for 14s.9d.

Representatives from across the county supported the resolution and when proposed by Graham Campbell of Shirvan it was unanimously resolved to send copies of the resolution to the Prime Minister, the Chancellor of the Exchequer, the Secretary for Scotland, the Board of Trade, the Caledonian Canal Commissioners and the Members of Parliament for all west of Scotland constituencies. A committee was set up to carry the scheme forward and to arrange a deputation to the

Secretary for Scotland. The problem was, as always, the cost of the plan, and the many recipients of the 1912 resolution seem to have simply ignored it – presumably in the hope that it would go away.

In the Argyll Archives at Inveraray Castle there is evidence that after two and a half years there had still been no response to the correspondence about the proposed ship canal. And, of course, by that time Great Britain was at war. Men were drafted, there was not enough labour to keep the existing canal in good order, and the puffers were using the canal on war business. They were commissioned to service the fleet at Scapa Flow, the stretch of water between the Orkney Islands that, following the experience gained during the Napoleonic Wars, was used as a safe haven for British ships. Defences were built there and the plucky little Clyde puffers braved the mined seas outside the 'safe' zone to take supplies to the men. But a war was not going to deter the ship canal petitioners from pursuing their cause – indeed, writing from Castle Lachlan in June 1915, MacLachlan of MacLachlan, convenor of Argyll County Council, pointed out that the 'usefulness' of the existing canal in war was 'curtailed by size and other defects'. The strategic value of a ship canal was being ignored, he claimed in a letter to the Rt Hon. James W. Lowther, the then chair of the Caledonian Canal Commissioners.

In the following year, those commissioners presented their 111th report for the year ending 30 April 1916. There had been no interruption to navigation on the Crinan Canal during 1915-16, although a very dry period from May to November 1915, with the rainfall 16-18 inches below the average of the previous 20 years, had meant water supplies were 'on several occasions' very nearly exhausted. Traffic and revenue returns were down every month on the previous year, with an annual revenue of £1,988.3s.2d recorded. The drop was due 'entirely to conditions resulting from the war' and the small number of craft able to use the canal. The report said that the Admiralty had requisitioned a high percentage of cargo boats regularly using the canal. While in 1914-15, 1,821 passengers had gone through the canal, in 1915-16, the figure was 1,053, of whom 52 were on Admiralty service. The receipts from all sources on 4 April 1915 had been £5,153.6s.8d. In April 1916, they were down to £3,775.10s.6d, including a loan from the Treasury of £500 to assist the finances of the canal to 'meet the deficit occasioned by the war'.

The financial situation was probably as bad as it had ever been, even though there had been that long period when the canal had broken even. The amount of stock held by the commissioners in respect of the Crinan Canal was £500, described as 4.5 per cent War Stock, 'representing an investment of the money previously on deposit with the Bank of Scotland'. There was a further depletion of staff because of enlistments, so no repairs were carried out that were 'not immediately necessary'. And as if it needed to be said, the report added that the canal was 'in no way improved'. An interesting note says, 'Government traffic on the Crinan Canal from the outbreak of war to April 30, 1916, if paid for at ordinary rates, would have produced a total revenue of £152, 10s 7d.' It can be assumed from this that the government also 'requisitioned' free passages through the canal.

L. John Groves, the engineer, reported that damage to Ardrishaig's breakwater caused by winter storms would have to be made good. Ahead of the next winter weather, it was proposed to beach the ice-breaker (which had only been used four times in 1915-16) in the harbour to scrape and paint the hull because of the great difficulty and expense of sending her to a slip on the Clyde. The dangers of war lurked in the Clyde estuary as well as up at Scapa Flow. With reservoirs emptying and Zeppelin raids 'getting a bit serious', this really wasn't a time to be pushing for a ship canal. The following year there would be submarines in the Clyde, and passengers on the mail boat arrived from Glasgow at Ardrishaig wearing their lifebelts, which sent those waiting with the intention of travelling to Glasgow 'fleeing from the pier'.

Even so, on 15 March 1917, with the war raging around them, and all the young men and some of the older ones away at the Front, and telegrams about fatalities arriving with terrible regularity, a meeting was held in the Court House, Lochgilphead, and a 'memorial' was put together by local proprietors, farmers and 'others interested in the development of agriculture in Argyllshire and the Western Isles'. It was to be sent to the Rt Hon. the Speaker of the House of Commons, and the chairman of the commissioners of the Caledonian and Crinan canals. It was prefaced by the desperate statement that it was the 'bounden duty of those assembled to commend the matter through you to the Commissioners of the Canal for earnest consideration'. The 'matter', of course, was the development of the Crinan Canal, which they admitted 'In the early days . . . was of the greatest possible use and a great blessing.' Now they gave it a lifetime of another three or four years – or a ship canal would replace it and all would be well again.

Just as Campbell of Islay had proposed using the starving men stricken by the potato famine in the 1840s to enlarge and modernise the canal, giving them money in their pockets and the canal a new lease on life, so the Lochgilphead assembly proposed a useful solution: 'How long the present War will last, it is impossible to say, but if the Reconstruction of the Canal could be taken in hand at once it was suggested that it could afford most suitable employment for a large number of German prisoners.'

Melville Neill, chair of the meeting, sent a copy of the proceedings to the Duke of Argyll on 5 May 1917, seeking his support, but even the duke was up against a range of problems that made this suggestion unlikely to garner success. From 1913 to 1921, debate about another canal was hogging the limelight: the Forth & Clyde Canal was seen as far more economically and strategically important to Scotland and to the country as a whole, and the Crinan Canal was sidelined as a priority.

However, there was discussion in parliament on 15 November 1917, when the April 1917 report of the commissioners was raised by Sir John Ainsworth, who asked the Secretary for Scotland if he was aware that numerous representations had reached the Caledonian Canal commissioners about the state of the Crinan Canal – stressing that the situation had 'repeatedly' been raised. The canal was now, Sir John said, in imminent danger of collapse and closure without some action. Mr Clyde, an MP and one of the Caledonian Canal commissioners, was asked to reply for the Secretary for Scotland (who had no responsibility for canals, it was stressed). The commissioners had, in fact, arranged a loan of around £7,500 for both the Caledonian and Crinan canals for the duration of the war 'to provide against the possibility of such breakdown as the Hon. Member has in mind'. When the war came to an end in 1918, many things changed, but there was no provision either for the Crinan Canal to be fully restored or for the plans for a ship canal to proceed. In

1919, the Ministry of Transport Act came onto the statute books and the Ministry of Transport (Commissioners of the Caledonian Canal Transfer of Powers and Property) Order 1920 brought both the Caledonian and Crinan canals into the hands of this new body. The commissioners ceased to exist.

16

Sink or swim?

The transfer to the Ministry of Transport may seem like a contradiction of all that the government had ever tried to do with this little canal in what Westminster still saw as the middle of nowhere. For a century and a quarter, government after government had washed its collective hands of the canal, lending money, making grants, dispensing admonitions to successive companies and commissioners to 'do better or else' – but always keeping responsibility for it at arm's length. Now it belonged to a very modern government department (so modern that there were many who didn't believe there was a need for it) that dealt with railways and roads and harbours and waterways. Would there be modern plans and solutions to the problems?

In 1928, there was a debate in the House of Commons about the construction of a tunnel under the Channel. There had been 'tunnel mania' in the latter part of the nineteenth century in the same way as there had been 'Railway Mania' in the 1840s (there had even been that exciting proposal to link Antrim and Kintyre by a rail tunnel). Perversely, having crippled the Crinan Canal by withholding adequate funding for a century, when the Channel Tunnel was proposed it was the Crinan Canal that was held up as the place where money should be spent. Prime Minister Stanley Baldwin was asked by Frederick Alexander Macquisten, MP for Glasgow Springburn, if he were 'not of the opinion that a much more useful expenditure of public money would be to remake the Crinan Canal?' Hansard, the official record of parliamentary proceedings, does not record Mr Baldwin's response. When the Channel Tunnel came up again later in June 1928, Mr Macquisten asked the Prime Minister to keep in mind that 'a Commission sat in 1878 ... and reported favourably on making the Crinan Ship Canal'. All the later plans and demands for a ship canal had come to nothing and, indeed, Mr Macquisten was valiantly flogging a dead canal track-horse.

However, the man was nothing if not persistent. In March 1930 when a Ministry of Transport debate looked into, among many other issues, advances made to the Caledonian and Crinan canals, it was clear that something had indeed to be done. There had been another closure because of water shortage. Herbert Morrison, Minister of Transport from 1929 to 1931, referred to the Caledonian Canal as one of his 'unprofitable possessions' (in 1930, it had suffered extensive damage), and it was pointed out that the bigger steamers now went round by the North Sea.

One MP said: 'Although there may be many who regret very much the passing of the Caledonian Canal, we have to face the fact that conditions in connection with transport have entirely changed since the canal was built, and if this is, as I suppose it is, a matter which we may have to face from year to year by being called upon to make additional payments, it becomes of value to know whether, in the interests of the fishing industry, for example, or of local trade, it is worth keeping the Caledonian Canal under the conditions which now exist.'

If Crinan's 'Big Brother' was so badly threatened, what of the Crinan? Unemployment in the post-war era was becoming an increasing problem. Questions were raised in this debate about plans for road bridges over the Tay and Forth as employment solutions, but a government has to have money to be able to alleviate the effects of a Depression and the British government was still recovering financially from the crippling effects of the Great War. The Crinan Canal's hero of the day, Mr Macquisten, believed both canals would benefit if money were granted to introduce labour schemes. He asked the minister, 'Why was the work outlined [for the canals] not proceeded with to help unemployment? I am not satisfied with the description of the canals as unprofitable possessions and as obsolete institutions. My contention is that Governments have never taken the trouble to develop them.' He was right, of course, but now was not the time for the government to be generous to the two canals. Indeed, when was?

There were objections in 1933 to money being spent on the Crinan Canal, but in November 1934, Leslie Hore-Belisha, the then Transport minister, said some outlay had indeed been made – an additional reservoir for supplying water to the canal had recently been provided.

As luck (or lack of it) would have it, there had again been Argyll's 'feast or famine' situation in relation to rainfall. It had been exceptionally low during the winter of 1933–34, and in the summer of 1934 the reservoirs supplying water to the canal had not filled. It had not, therefore, been possible to take advantage of the additional storage capacity made available by the provision of the new reservoir. The minister believed the new reservoir would in the future provide adequate reserves to keep the canal open. Mr Macquisten kept plugging away on the old girl's behalf, demanding in 1937 how long the canal would have to stay closed after a laden vessel seriously damaged the sea gates. He received the written reply that re-opening depended on the gate sluice castings being received from a company in Glasgow, but that extra men had been employed in the canal workshops. Macquisten must have felt like a voice crying in the wilderness, but at last the canal was not going to rack and ruin.

While there is a negative thread still running through all of these parliamentary negotiations, the sun had shone on the canal after the First World War. Indeed, there is a photograph of RMS *Columba* and *Iona* delivering a full complement of passengers to Ardrishaig in 1917, a full year before the end of the war. The popular *Linnet* had continued to ply between Ardrishaig and Crinan until 1929, and then, despite all the objections in parliament, there was a major reconstruction in the early 1930s, when locks and bridges were upgraded and approaches deepened. But just as steam led to vessels that were too big for the canal from the first quarter of the nineteenth century, so were there dramatic transport changes at the beginning of the twentieth. In 1929, MacBrayne replaced the Crinan Canal steamer, but, more drastic in terms of the future of the canal, the Crinan to Oban steamer was replaced by a motor coach that ran direct between Ardrishaig and Oban. This was, of course, progress. People wanted to reach their destinations faster. The railways had been taking people to Inverness from the Central Belt since the nineteenth century – they didn't need to go via two canals on three boats. The railway to Oban from Glasgow took away the need to travel through the Clyde estuary to reach the West Highland town. It had been scarcely a village when Victoria and Albert sailed there. Now it was the 'Gateway to the

Islands' and people got off a train and onto a ferry to reach those islands.

Society changed much more quickly in the twentieth century. Provision for a form of old-age pension was introduced before the First World War, and even in 1912 there was a question in the House of Commons about whether Crinan Canal workers would be entitled (working, as they now did, for a government-owned operation) '. . . to an incapacitated allowance of 5s. per week on their retiral on account of old age, in view of the fact that they have been working on the understanding that half-wage would be paid them in such circumstances?' The answer was that they would be entitled to five shillings a week disablement benefit if they were incapable of work under the ordinary conditions of the Insurance Act. Workmen had been given half-wages during temporary illnesses, not as permanent allowances. Pensions for long service had been, and would be, considered on the individual merits of each case; and would not be discontinued in consequence of the Insurance Act. Whatever the mechanics of developing pension schemes, Alasdair Blair, who was born into a 'canal' family in 1930 and spent his working life as a member of the Crinan lock keepers' team, remembered the system of tied houses which had to be vacated on retirement at 65 – a sadness for most, who kept beautiful gardens and had to leave these behind. The parliamentary debates of the first part of the twentieth century suggest an ailing waterway with a failing present and little hope of a future, but Mr Blair remembered a childhood filled with fishing boats and puffers, and even a burgeoning tourist industry, albeit the Crinan Hotel catered for those who motored to Mid Argyll rather than sailed there. Guests could hire one of four or five boats owned by the hotel, and the boats were kept spick and span during the winter by two elderly brothers who scraped and painted them. It was still a time of barter – the fishermen left baskets of fish and the crews from the boats were given eggs and vegetables from the lock keepers' gardens.

The canal's circumstances seemed to change so little – witness an exchange in parliament in November 1934 when Mr Joseph Leckie MP asked the Secretary of State for Scotland what steps were being taken 'to prevent a recurrence of the closing of the Crinan Canal in the month of July last, owing to shortage of water, in view of the inconvenience then caused'. That same old problem was met with a reply from Mr Hore-Belisha, who told the House that an additional reservoir for supplying water to the canal had recently been provided, but 'owing to the exceptionally low rainfall during the winter of 1933-34 and the last summer, the reservoirs supplying water to the canal have not filled'. The additional storage capacity had not been of use so far, but it should, it was thought, provide adequate supplies of water in the future. And there were the boats that, as they had since the outset, damaged the lock and seagates with monotonous regularity, causing canal closures – one such incident in June 1937 meant a month-long closure and extra men shipped in from Glasgow to deal with the engineering repairs.

The scenery, however, did begin to change with the planting of conifers in the 1930s. The Forestry Act of 1919 set out to provide the country with adequate timber stocks following natural decline and the demands of war. In the 1930s agriculture, as with other sectors, was still in depression and the Forestry Commission took on more and more land for timber cultivation. The sheep and cattle that had dominated the hillsides of the Crinan Canal began to disappear as the plantations took hold. Kilmahumaig had been a thriving sheep farm and there were others on the hills behind Bellanoch. Horses did the ploughing still – the first tractor in the area arrived to great excitement in the mid-1930s. This change in the landscape did not deter the visitors, who ranged from those who paid 7s.6d for bed and breakfast and 5s for an evening meal in a local house to those who required a 'boots', a chauffeur-driven hire car and a top-class chef at the Crinan Hotel. Local wages were £4 a week, so such extra income was very welcome. Although the *Linnet* (which had carried up to 301 passengers along the canal on their two hours and forty minute jaunt) had been pensioned off, Caledonian MacBrayne boats still brought people in their droves to Ardrishaig and many would travel on Andrew Grimshaw's coach for a hurl around the local countryside. Transport for the canal workers was a bike.

Money was spent on the canal, despite those in parliament who always were ready to say 'no'. Locks were reconstructed and deepened in the 1930s, but it was still seen as remote and pretty useless. In 1940, parliament was told that the average annual income from dues for the Crinan Canal for the years 1930 to 1939 had been approximately £6,100. There were four of a staff supervising and controlling the canal and there were 12 permanent lock keepers who were paid between 41s and 48s a week. They were to receive a four shillings a week rise, and of course their tied houses were rent-free and each lock keeper was issued with waterproof clothing. Men like James Purdie, who worked on the canal in the later twentieth century, recalled that in a previous generation between 80 and 100 people worked on the maintenance of the canal, but, according to the records, this must have been on a temporary basis to meet specific repair work.

As the Second World War broke out, the canal took on an importance it had experienced a number of times in its history. This time, communication was a little faster and clearer. In September 1939, a telegram was sent from the Admiralty in London ordering navigation lights to be extinguished – a pre-arranged operation planned in secret in August 1938. Although some lock keepers were called up for active service, some were retained to keep the canal open. There were army and naval bases on Loch Fyne and Admiralty vessels used the canal. HMS *Seahawk* was a Second World War Royal Navy shore establishment at Ardrishaig, responsible primarily for anti-submarine training, commissioned on 1 January 1941. Midget submarines used the canal as a route to their work attacking the German Fleet in the Atlantic, and training continued in the area until 1944. With coal in short supply during the war, that old bartering system proved a life-saver as the puffers continued to drop off 'surplus' fuel in exchange for vegetables from the lock keepers' gardens. With fish supplementing their diet, it could seem as if those working on the canal had an easy war – but the German air command saw it as a main artery leading from the industrial belt, as well as a route for military and naval manoeuvres. A bomb was dropped on Bellanoch, causing huge anxiety but little damage. The banks of the Crinan Canal also became host to prisoners of war. The POW camp was near Lock 8 at Cairnbaan, where there were around 20 wooden huts and a Nissen hut. The camp (now the site of Letter Daill private housing complex and Forestry Commission workshops) housed Italian and German prisoners, who made wooden toys for the local children. Soldiers in charge of the camps brought the toys into the little school at Cairnbaan, where between 20 and 30 pupils continued their primary education.

The Cairnbaan Hotel (one of those that grew out of the early days of the canal's existence), a post office and Cairnbaan Stores provided local people with most necessities, and vans with other provisions toured the length of the canal to serve all its inhabitants. As always, life went on for those who worked the canal and plied its waters. Life was rarely easy and the money was never good, but the memories of those who spent their childhoods or their working lives on the Crinan Canal are good ones. Who owned the canal, who financed it, who made decisions about it were details that did not (and had not since its earliest days) impinge on day-to-day living. So, when in 1947 the Crinan and Caledonian canals were transferred to the British Transport Commission it was just one more set of bosses. There were still puffers called *Kaffir* and *Zulu* plying the canal, still droughts and deluges plaguing its supply of water, still clumsy skippers scraping their vessels off lock gates.

And then came nationalisation. In 1948, transport was nationalised, bringing canals, docks and ships belonging to railway companies under the newly established British Transport Commission. The Crinan Canal was part of the process. Yet again, it seemed that it was more likely to sink than swim. Life was changing again in so many ways and this rural Scottish backwater seemed useless to cargo and fishing boats as the 1950s progressed. However, if the working boats were using the routes that had once seemed too hazardous, the leisure craft were beginning to ply the waters of the Clyde and the Crinan and Caledonian canals in greater numbers. Ever-bigger ships had been avoiding the Crinan Canal since the *Comet*, and had long since ceased to seem a threat to its continued operation – at local level, at least. When the British Waterways Board took the canal over under the Transport

Act, 1962, commercial use may well have been in continued decline, but now, with its leaks repaired and at long last the tourist potential initiated by Queen Victoria recognised, the canal began to flourish as a destination, not just a waterway on the way to somewhere else.

17

Very definitely swimming

It took a while to adjust to the fact that tourists had their own agenda. The yachts may have headed towards the Crinan Canal in the 1960s and '70s, but that wasn't to say they were warmly welcomed. Alex Howie, who became a lock keeper at that time, has said that the canal was geared solely to the needs of the working vessel and no concessions were made to pleasure craft. Indeed, the canal closed on Saturdays and Sundays – the very time when, by definition, pleasure craft wanted to access it. With the increasing decline in the number of puffers and fishing boats travelling through the waterway, things had to change. It wasn't easy to adjust after 170 years to a new working pattern, but as Mondays and Tuesdays became the canal workers' 'weekend', things began to look up.

It had been over a century since Victoria and Albert had sailed through the canal on the *Sunbeam* and set a tourist trend. The Royal Route had its heyday and there had been the *Linnet*'s populist day-tripper era, but both were subservient to what was seen as the 'real' work of the canal – to provide a passage for cargo and fishing boats heading north and west from the Clyde. Now there had to be a rethink. Always subject to the 'too small' accusation, the Crinan Canal had to think modern, to think 'small is beautiful'. Although there had never been any argument about the attractiveness of the waterway, another facelift for the heroine of our drama had to be carefully designed. Danny Kennedy was the man for the job, and it is to be hoped that along with the other names that have become associated with the Crinan Canal – Watt, Rennie and Telford – that Kennedy will also be remembered. Waterways manager from 1989 to 2005, he was charged with the task of turning round the canal's fortunes. There was nothing new in the fact that outgoings far outweighed income – it was ever thus – but Kennedy was not content to accept the status quo. Around £300,000 was all that was being raised by canal dues. More than double that was being spent on its maintenance. The vision was that the canal could attract huge tourist revenues to the area, and Kennedy was willing to take a risk – close the canal for three months, and use modern strategies to achieve the dream. Together with Alex Howie, Kennedy convinced the canal bosses that Ardrishaig, Bellanoch and Crinan should be modernised to meet the tourists' needs. The old ploys to convince investors to buy into the first canal plans had worked, but marketing strategies had moved on since the later eighteenth century and the hard sell to bring visitors to the new marinas paid off.

The 30-year-engineering plan (no sticking plaster solutions now, as in the early days) aimed not only to upgrade the canal but also to care for the environment while bringing in revenue. The facelift carried out in the 1990s included conservation and biodiversity elements, and the clever bit was to develop a timber transportation centre at Ardrishaig. The plan added to the £7 million tourist income without impinging on the attractions of this 'most beautiful shortcut in Britain', and the timber transportation centre has grown from handling 30,000 tonnes each year to 150,000 tonnes – an important part of Scotland's timber trade. Kennedy knew that the canal would never be self-sufficient – an admission few had made publicly in the past. He knew it would always leak. He knew there would always be a need for expensive maintenance. He knew the three-month closure to improve facilities was a risk, but he made no apologies for that or for spending cash on the canal. 'If you want a future for the canal, what is a three month closure against permanent closure?' he demanded.

Some things (like the leaks) won't ever change. That lack of pozzolana back at the beginning, thanks to Napoleon's shenanigans, was just one of the reasons why the Crinan Canal would never be perfect. The Argyll weather may become even more unpredictable because of climate change, and we have seen the devastating effects on the canal of both too much rain and too little. Some things are a little different, however. Less severe winters mean there is no need for icebreaker boats such as the *Conway*, with its big metal ribs on the bow to cut through the ice and allow the puffers and fishing boats through. And while diving bells were used from the early nineteenth century to carry out underwater repairs, followed by divers using the old Siebe Gorman system (they used massive brass helmets, canvas and leather suits, and heavy boots, and were let down to the bottom of the canal, accessing air through a tube to the surface where a man pumped bellows on the towpath), today it is contract divers who do the underwater work three or four times a year. The Glenfyne Distillery disappeared. In its last years it was used as a hatchery for salmon smolts, some of which escaped into the canal. The water is clean enough for a whole range of wildlife, including salmon and trout, which are stunned, removed, and then returned to their habitat when the canal is drained for repairs. Some 5,000 fish are conserved this way and the process is part of the modern canal's budget. The environment matters.

Today, the Crinan Canal is in the hands of Scottish Canals. In the twenty-first century, an ever-greater emphasis has been placed on providing accessibility to the canal – not only for boats but walkers, bikers and horse riders. There are those, including this writer, who feel that Scottish Canals can be over-zealous in their efforts to provide accessibility. In 2016, a grant has enabled the organisation to drown the towpaths in a surfeit of tarmacadam. It reflects a certain insensitivity to historical authenticity, and we can only hope that racing cyclists don't take advantage of the resulting speedway. The Dalriada Project, in partnership with Argyll & Bute Council, Forestry Commission Scotland, British Waterways Scotland, the Waterways Trust Scotland, Scottish Natural Heritage, the Scottish Wildlife Trust and Kilmartin House Museum, has created walkways, provided podcasts and signage, and enhanced the experience of both visitor and local residents alike. These improvements are so much more in keeping with the spirit of the canal in the twenty-first century, and a planned consultation with the community will hopefully tip the balance back to harmony with nature and respect for all canal users.

The MacTavishes of Dunardry wouldn't recognise the place: there is now a nature trail through ancient Atlantic oak woodlands to the Crinan Canal at Dunardry. John Paterson, the engineer, would be lost if he took a walk along the towpath, where so many improvements have been made. For the twenty-first-century visitor, however, there is not only unobtrusive but informative signage interpreting the landscape. There are also the ghosts of Crinan Canal past: layers of human endeavour, enterprise, engineering innovation and achievement. There is a sense of the heartaches, the suffering inflicted by wars, famines and floods. There are the ghosts of those who stayed and those who left on boats for America.

The one thing that might never have been expected from the chequered history of this stretch of water is an award. Despite the illustrious names associated with the Crinan Canal, that constant refrain of 'too small, too late', the carping of the politicians, the neglect and the constant drain on the public purse all conspire to suggest that the star of this show was never going to be given the Oscar. And yet, in October 2015, plaques were unveiled at Ardrishaig and Crinan by the Institution of Civil Engineers, acknowledging the engineering achievement of the Crinan Canal. At the ceremony, Alan Frew, chairman of the ICE Glasgow and West of Scotland Branch, said, 'The engineering achievement of the Crinan Canal cannot be underestimated, particularly in light of the many problems overcome by the project during its inception more than 200 years ago . . . The Crinan really is a magnificent feat of engineering.'

A technical epilogue

Agreeing that this may not have been the ideal site for a canal in technical terms, geologist Dr Roger Anderton has kindly looked at some of the engineering geology of the Crinan Canal, dividing it into five construction sections. The first runs from Ardrishaig to Badden, just north of Lochgilphead, and is retained by a high embankment running along the coast. The second stretch is from Badden to Lock 5 at Cairnbaan, which he described as a level section running along the edge of the Craiglass Meadows and retained by a lower embankment. The third section is from Lock 5 to Lock 13 near Barnakill Farm, described by Dr Anderton as 'the heavily locked section, which includes the summit level . . . largely cut into the valley bottom'. The fourth section is from Lock 13 to the road junction south-east of Kilmahumaig, a level section retained by another high embankment along the Add estuary. Finally, the fifth section runs from the Kilmahumaig junction to Crinan, 'a section characterised by deep rock cuttings as well as a high embankment'.

Dr Anderton explained that in the first section, the canal has been cut into the natural east-facing hill slope and that the east side is retained 'by an impressive embankment'. From there, the canal climbs to an elevation of about ten to 11 metres, thereafter continuing on that level to Lock 5 at Cairnbaan. A narrow natural rock platform along the western side of Loch Gilp, around 100 to 150 metres wide, and five to seven metres above sea level, is backed by a steeper slope and can still be seen south of the canal entrance. Dr Anderton identifies this as the surface on which today's main road and some neighbouring houses are built. This platform was cut towards the end of the last Ice Age, about 12,000 years ago, when the sea level was higher. It is a feature sometimes known as a raised beach. The canal, according to Dr Anderton, was constructed by digging a trench into the back of this platform, where the ground starts to steepen. The spoil was cast forward to form the embankment.

Although this first section of the canal did not seem to cause too many problems during the initial construction, Dr Anderton identifies rock exposed on the foreshore at many points just south of the canal entrance northwards along the shore of Loch Gilp and he says this 'must underlie the canal at a shallow depth'. He adds, 'As shown by Smith's 1823 map, a gap in this shallow bedrock, which previously formed a small bay, has been exploited to form the canal entrance'. Today's timber wharf is built on another rocky area.

This first area of construction must have been expensive, as the cost of explosives rose in the wartime situation. Dr Anderton explained that rock is exposed in the curved back wall of the basin between the sea lock and Lock 2, 'where it has been chiselled to form a smooth surface'. Rock continues between Locks 2 and 3, and 100 to 200 metres north of Lock 4 in front of the houses Elmwood and Elmbank. Below Elmbank the rock is exposed in the canal bank itself and Dr Anderton suggested, 'It is likely that much of this reach was cut into the bedrock.' More rock is visible on the west side of the canal between Glendarroch and Oakfield, 'in particular where there are spurs in the hillside which have been cut across in an attempt to keep the canal as straight as possible'. The effect is a narrowing of the canal from the general width of 24 to 28 metres to between 14 and 18 metres, 'where it bends more sharply and cuts across the apex of these spurs'.

The rock is largely green phyllite (metamorphosed siltstone and mudstone), which Dr Anderton said is not a particularly hard rock, but within it are harder bands of pale quartzite (metamorphosed sandstone), such as seen in front of Elmbank, and metabasite (metamorphosed dolerite intrusions). He added: 'All these rocks are cut by closely-spaced natural fracture planes (a combination of bedding, cleavage, joints and faults) which would have facilitated the quarrying and removal of the rock. All these rocks are together known as the Ardrishaig Phyllite Formation.'

Dr Anderton suggested that the engineers designed the canal so that the amount of material excavated to form the three-metre trench would equal that required to form the embankment, although as we have seen weather conditions meant that almost as soon as the canal was opened, extra material was frequently required to consolidate the embankments throughout the length of the canal. Dr Anderton estimated that some four to eight million cubic feet would have been excavated (some of it rock, some clay, sand or gravel) and, given that a navvy could shift around seven tons a day, 'the process of moving this material would require about 50,000 man-days of work, say 100 men for 500 days'. We know that in 1794 Lachlan MacTavish wrote to his relative Coll Lamont of Moneydrain that 400 men had 'already done wonders' by November of that year, extending the canal beyond Lamont's property. The letter supports Dr Anderton's assumption that a workforce of 'hundreds rather than thousands of men' was needed.

The bedrock in the Craiglass Meadows section comprises

quartzites and grits (metamorphosed sandstones and conglomerates) and slates (metamorphosed mudstones) of the Crinan Grit Formation. Dr Anderton commented that these rocks produce a more varied landscape than seen in the first section of the canal, with spurs and valleys modifying the general east to north-easterly hill slope. 'Bedrock is seen in the canal bank where it cuts across a spur at NR 8493 8967 and both Langland's (1794) and Smith's (1823) maps imply that the canal was designed to cut across other rocky spurs to the north.'

He explained that although the material under the Meadows is not known, if it is similar to the Crinan Moss (Mòine Mhòr) then below the surface peat layer there should be sand and gravel, then clay, before the bedrock is reached. He said: 'These superficial deposits are geologically recent, having accumulated since the peak of the last Ice Age, in comparison to the bedrock which is over 600 million years old. These deposits, especially if waterlogged, are likely to be much weaker and more susceptible to failure than those underlying the canal to the south. It is not surprising, therefore, to find that this is the section that suffered a major bank failure.'

Dr Anderton spotted that rather than repair the breach on the north-east side of the canal, the engineers rebuilt the canal to the west, forming a diversion over 500 metres long and running along the very edge of the Meadows, rather than taking a short cut across it. Dr Anderton believed that this implies that the soft superficial sediments failed under the weight of the embankment because they would have been much thinner. 'They may even have been totally excavated so that a firmer foundation could be laid for the embankment.'

In the next (and most troublesome) section of the canal, Dr Anderton suggested that the canal construction diverted

A TECHNICAL EPILOGUE

a number of streams. The Dunardry burn, for example, according to the Langland's map, had originally flowed along the line of the small reservoir adjacent to the small basin containing the *Linnet* shed, and another small stream had flowed along the north side of the canal to the south of a house called Woodglen and through the site now occupied by Loch a'Bharain. This joined the Dunardry burn at the position now occupied by the basin between Locks 9 and 10. The combined drainage then flowed through Lock 10 into the next basin before turning north into the valley between the canal and Barnakill Farm, then heading along the present course of the Barnakill Burn into the Add.

Did that terrible landslide in the middle of the nineteenth century destroy the courses of these streams? Were they altered to accommodate the *Linnet* shed? Did the construction of other reservoirs change nature's routes? At this distance we can only speculate and examine the early maps.

The expertise of the geologist, the precision of the early cartographers, and the written reports of a succession of site engineers have all helped to preserve so much of the history of this tiny canal. The human element – the characters who shaped it in so many different ways – and the forces of nature that have also lent drama that few other canals, large or small, have experienced, make this not just the most beautiful shortcut in Britain but one of the most fascinating.

Acknowledgements

The wealth of documents that have informed this book were made available with imagination and enthusiasm by the hugely helpful staff at a number of archive centres.

I would like to thank most sincerely Jackie Davenport, the archives officer for Argyll and Bute Council, and her assistant, Rory Crutchfield, who patiently worked around the basic 'Crinan Canal' concept to come up with relevant correspondence and information held in many other files in their Lochgilphead premises.

There was a similarly imaginative and comprehensive approach taken by Ishbel MacKinnon, archivist at Argyll Estates in Inveraray, where I found material about the wars and famines that affected the local population and the construction and maintenance of the canal.

The customary efficiency of the staff at the National Records of Scotland in Edinburgh made it possible to make best use of an economically viable number of visits from Mid Argyll to the capital, and I am grateful to Josephine Dixon, Samantha Smart and others, who were all most thorough in their search for appropriate documents.

Because of the close association with the Caledonian Canal, a visit to Inverness was necessary, where Colin Waller, archivist at Highlife Highland, Highland Archive Centre, organised access to still more essential documents.

Chris O'Connell, information management and heritage officer at Scottish Canals' office in Glasgow, clearly shared my enthusiasm for the history of the canal and provided not only fascinating documents but also some splendid maps and an Admiralty telegram.

Argyll artist Lesley Burr introduced me to her friend Clare Gent – a serendipitous meeting that brought to light not only new maps but also some beautiful elevation drawings of the canal that had been rescued by her father, Terence Gent, who had worked for British Rail and was also a parliamentary assistant. The family is not sure if the drawings came from BR offices that were clearing out items in the late 1970s and early 1980s that were 'no longer deemed useful', or whether they were rescued during site visits when there were changes to land use connected with what the railway owned. I can only thank Clare for sharing these beautiful items.

Thanks also to Eleanor McKay, information and local studies librarian, Argyll and Bute Library Service, who provided more images of the Crinan Canal from the collection of the late Archie Campbell of Ardrishaig.

The patient work of my editor at Birlinn, Deborah Warner, is sincerely appreciated.

I would also like to thank Charlotte Brodie Eastin for information about her ancestor Murdoch Brodie, or Broddie, and his family. Murdoch was an early Crinan Canal lock keeper and Charlotte's research into her family history proved most useful for my own researches.

Bibliography

Books and Articles

Aiton, W. *A treatise on the origin, qualities, and cultivation of moss-earth: with directions for converting it into manure, published at the request of and under the patronage of the Highland Society of Scotland* (Ayr: Wilson & Paul, 1811)

Anonymous, 'The Destruction of the Crinan Canal', *Illustrated London News*, 5 March 1859, p. 233

Bradford, E.F. *MacTavish of Dunardry* (Whitby: E.F. Bradford, 1991)

Campbell Byatt, Fiona, 'From Russia to Lochgilphead: the Keirs in the 19th Century', *The Kist*, Vol. 90 (FSA Scot, 2015), pp. 13-21

Cross-Rudkin, P. *Canal Contractors 1760–1820* http://www.rchs.org.uk/trial/J207_27%20Canal%20Contractors.pdf [Last accessed 12 October 2015]

Crouch & Hogg, *Memorandum on the Proposed Ship Canal from Loch Gilp to Loch Crinan* (Glasgow, University Press, 1896)

Dick, Alexander J. 'On the Financial Crisis, 1825-26' in *BRANCH: Britain, Representation and Nineteenth-Century History*, Dino Franco Felluga (ed.). Extension of *Romanticism and Victorianism on the Net*. Web. [Last accessed 15 November 2015]

Duff, D. (ed.) *Queen Victoria's Highland Journals* (Exeter: Webb & Bower, 1980)

Fleetwood, D. 'Power to the People: the built heritage of Scotland's hydroelectric power', http://www.historic-scotland.gov.uk/power-to-the-people.pdf [Last accessed 15 December 2015]

Harrison, J.G. Heavy Metal Mines in the Ochil Hills: Chronology and Context http://www.johnscothist.com/uploads/5/0/2/4/5024620/ochils_mines_and_minerals.pdf [Last accessed 13 September 2015]

Hills, Rev. Dr Richard L. *James Watt, Volume 1: His time in Scotland, 1736–1774* (Ashbourne: Landmark, 2002)

Morrison, Professor A. 'The Defence of Scotland – Militias, Fencibles and Volunteer Corps 1793-1820', 9 October 2011, http://www.scribd.com/doc/68100606/The-Defence-of-Scotland-Militias-Fencibles-and-Volunteer-Corps1793-1820#scribd [Last accessed 12 August 2015]

'Scotland', http://archive.spectator.co.uk/article/12th-february-1859/5/scotland [Last accessed 7 December 2015]

Williams, Lee 'Britain and banking: Back to the 1830s', last updated 12 July 2012 http://blogs.independent.co.uk/2012/07/12/britain-and-banking-back-to-the-1830s/ [Last accessed 7 December 2015]

Reports and Papers

Reports from Committees, Caledonian and Crinan Canals: Volume III, 1839 https://books.google.co.uk/books?id=5XFbAAAAQAAJ&printsec=frontcover&dq=Reports+from+Committees+Caledonian+and+Crinan+Canals&hl=en&sa=X&ved=0ahUKEwiw-976-pzKAhVD_w4KHcpqB2cQ6AEIIDAA#v=onepage&q=Reports%20from%20Committees%20Caledonian%20and%20Crinan%20Canals&f=false [Last accessed 15 December 2015]

Parliamentary Papers: 1780–1849, Volume 8, Part 1, 1839, HM Stationery Office, https://books.google.co.uk/books?id=jvBDAQAAMAAJ [Last accessed 15 December 2015]

Parliamentary Papers, House of Commons and Command, Volume 30, HM Stationary Office, 1864 https://books.google.co.uk/books?id=2e8SAAAAYAAJ&pg=PP14&dq=Crinan+Canal+Parliamentary+Papers [Last accessed 14 December 2015]

Volumes of Hansard http://hansard.millbanksystems.com/

Websites

History of Ardrishaig: http://www.ardrishaig.com/ardrishaigpages/historya1.htm [Last accessed 15 November 2015]

Index

Aberdeen 109, 137, 138
Achnashelloch (also 'Achinshelloch') 31
Add (River and Island Add) 31, 37, 56, 72, 107, 193, 194, 195, 223, 227
Aird, John 79, 82–3, 86, 90
Aiton, William 37, 38
Albert, HRH Prince 159–63, 164, 169, 181, 211, 218
Anderton, Dr Roger 13, 223–7
Antrim 191, 208
Appin 30, 130
Archangel 67
Ardrishaig 1, 31, 33, 41, 42, 51, 62, 63, 64, 70, 91, 97, 123, 137, 146, 147, 148–9, 166, 172, 175, 181–3, 185, 187, 192, 200, 204, 211, 214, 215, 219, 222, 223
Arkwright, Richard 14

Armstrong, Sir William 194
Arran 63, 67
Auchendarroch 41, 224, 184
Ayr (Ayrshire) 65, 67, 156

Badden 192, 193, 223
Baddenoch 69
Baillie, Evan 171
Ballachuilish 30
Balmoral 159
Baltic, 26, 29, 39, 125, 171
Banks, George 127
Bardarroch 36, 37, 44, 71
Barindaff (also Barrandaimh) 36
Baring, F.T. (Secretary to the Treasury) 148
Barinluaskin (also Barnluasgan) 36
Barnakil 112, 193, 223, 227
Barnard, Alfred 186–90
Bath 30
Belfast 67

Bell, Henry 121–2, 123
Bellanoch 36, 59–60, 69, 71, 73–4, 97, 140, 214, 215, 219
Ben Cruachan 70
Birmingham 8, 19, 33, 34, 63, 108
Black Eagle 162
Black, Joseph 14
Blaeu, Joan 41
Blair, Alasdair 212
Bond, James 10
Boston 20
Boswell, James 15, 47
Boulton and Watt 8, 9, 104
Boulton, Matthew 9, 19, 34, 121,
Braunston Tunnel 103
Breadalbane (John Campbell, fourth Earl and 1st Marquess) 1, 22, 30, 105
Bristol 26
British Aluminium Company 195, 202
Brocket, Andrew 61, 62
Brodie, George 120–1, 140
Brodie, Murdoch (and family) 119–21, 140
Bunessan 202
Burns, Robert 21, 47

Cairnbaan 43, 62, 63, 70, 71, 115, 166, 168, 183, 192–4, 215–16, 223,
Cairnbaan Hotel 115
Cairncross and Cairns 50
Caldwell, David 124
Caledonian Canal 10, 77, 97, 117, 118, 119, 123–4, 127–8, 130–1, 132, 133, 135, 136, 137, 139, 144, 145, 150, 162, 170, 171, 175, 176, 178, 181, 202, 203, 206, 207, 209, 216
Caledonian MacBrayne 214
Campbell, Alan 184
Campbell, Alexander 171
Campbell, Alexander of Auchendarroch 184
Campbell, Colonel John of Barbreck 36
Campbell, Duncan of Lochnell 54
Campbell, John (Malcolms' factor) 112
Campbell, John (Malcolms' lawyer) 112
Campbell, John Francis of Islay 155–7, 160, 164
Campbell, Lord John 33

Campbell, Marion of
Kilberry 38
Campbell, Messrs Archibald
and Duncan Campbell,
Greenock 32
Campbell, Revd Mr
Archibald 23
Campbell, Revd Mr Dugald
23
Campbell, Revd Mr Hugh
23, 24
Campbell, Rt Hon Lord
Frederick 33, 105
Campbell, Sir Donald 142–5
Campbell-Orde 184
Campbeltown (and
Campbelton) 19, 30,
65, 108, 113, 162
Canna (Isle of) 66, 67,
Cape Wrath 78
Carlisle 119
Castle Lachlan 203
Cathcart (Charles Schaw,
9th Lord Cathcart) 2–3,
4–5, 7, 33–4, 52
Catherine II, Empress of
Russia 34
Charles Parsons and
Company 197
Charles Stuart 1
Charlotte, HM Queen 34
Chesme Palace 34

Chevalier 181, 182
Clyde (Firth of Clyde &
Clyde ports) 6, 13, 26,
27, 29, 45, 66, 109,
123, 128, 129, 139,
182, 183, 197, 201,
203, 205, 211, 216
Clyde puffer 185
Coleridge, Samuel Taylor 16
Columba 186, 187, 211
Comet 8, 60, 121–3, 125,
216
Cork 67
Corpach 145
Cowan, John 140
Cragside (Northumberland)
204
Craiglass 101, 223, 225–6
Craignish 55, 123
Crinan (village and harbour;
also Creinan, Creenan,
Crianan and Portree)
7, 18, 19, 21, 22, 23,
25, 27, 29, 31, 38, 39,
45, 46, 50, 51, 55, 56,
57, 59, 60, 62, 63, 69,
71, 72, 74, 90, 93, 97,
98, 107, 109, 111, 123,
125, 137, 145, 147,
148, 149, 158, 162,
166, 168, 174, 182,
184, 186, 192, 195,

197, 198, 211, 219, 222, 223, 226
Crinan Ferry 37, 74
Crinan Hotel 212, 214
Crinan Moss (also Mòine Mhòr) 38, 174, 190, 193, 226
Crinan Ship Canal 191–203, 205, 206, 209
Cross-Rudkin, Peter 76–7
Crouch and Hogg 191, 192–6, 198
Culloden 1, 2, 53
Cumberland (Duke of) 2
Cunard, Samuel 158
Cunard, William 158

Dalkeith 5
David Hutcheson & Co. 181
Davis, Joseph Gordon 184
Dell (The 'Dell Passage' or 'Dell Route' and Daill) 31, 35, 43, 115, 190, 215
Dewar, Captain Donald 191
Dick, Alexander 151
Dnieper-Bug Canal (Royal Canal) 67
Drumlanrig 61
Drumlemble 19
Drummond, John 140

Dublin 67
Duke of Argyll (George, 6th Duke of) 116, 126
Duke of Argyll (George, 8th) 155, 159
Duke of Argyll (John, 5th) 1–2, 6, 19, 22, 28, 30, 33, 40–1, 47, 51–2, 53, 65, 105, 159, 182
Duke of Argyll (John, 7th) 150
Duke of Argyll (John, 9th) 202
Duke of Argyll (Niall, 10th) 206
Dumfries 21, 67, 109
Dunadd 33, 43
Dunamuck 62, 63, 71
Dunans 36, 37
Dunardry 31, 36–7, 38, 40, 43–4, 49–50, 59, 72, 73, 75, 79, 89, 94, 98, 101, 115, 137, 138, 175
Dunardry burn 227
Duntrune (also 'Duntroon') 31, 33, 35, 38, 39, 45, 47, 112, 190

Easdale (and Slate Islands) 30, 32, 132, 142, 186
East Linton 8

INDEX

Edinburgh 3, 8, 15, 16, 30, 31, 36, 109, 128, 133, 134, 139, 142, 148, 152, 186
Ellice, Edward 171
Eskdale 10

The Fairy 161
Falkirk 2, 172
Ferrier, John 95, 96
Flanders 2
Fort Augustus 194
Fort William 6, 78, 81, 97, 123, 129, 130, 162, 181
Forth and Clyde Canal 6, 206
Foyers 202
Freebairn, Charles 3–4
French, Colonel Fitzstephen MP 176
Frew, Alan 222

Gardner, William 62
George III, King 54
Gibraltar 21, 53
Gibson Craig, William 171
Gigha (island of) 198
Gillies, William 189
Gladstone, William 177
Glasgow 27, 33, 52, 65, 109, 123, 129, 145, 148, 185, 188, 191, 195, 197, 199, 200, 202, 205, 209, 211, 213
Glassary (and Kilmichael Glassary) 23, 45, 172
Glen Clachaig 114, 165
Glendarroch 186, 187, 189, 190, 224
Goulburn, Henry 126
Gow, James 37, 38, 108, 109–11
Gower, Lady Elizabeth Leveson 159
Graham, Colonel Humphrey 33, 43, 49, 54–5, 69–71, 83, 86, 96, 99–102, 107
Grand Junction Canal 103
Grangemouth 65
Grant, James Murray 171
Great Glen 77, 78, 118
Greenock 7, 32, 63, 65, 93, 122, 160, 186
Grenadier 187
Grey, Sir George 155
Grimshaw, Andrew 214
Groves, L. John 196, 204

Halifax (Canada) 67
Hamburg 67
Harrison, John G. 4
Hartley, L.P. 39
Helensburgh 122

Henry Hoey & Co. 186
Herbert, Charles 169, 173
Hollinsworth, James 102–7, 114, 116
Homer, Revds Arthur, William, & Philip 27
Hooker, Sir William 184
Hope, James 128, 133–6, 139, 147
Hore-Belisha, Leslie 210, 213
Howie, Alex 218, 219
Hume, David 14
Hungerford 61
Hutcheson, Alexander 182
Hutcheson, David 182

Inveraray 15, 28, 33, 47, 122, 129, 159, 160
Inverness 6, 123, 129, 133, 145, 148, 172, 181, 211
Iona 181, 182, 187, 211
Iona 30, 130, 162
Irvine 67
Islay 4, 18, 155, 160, 164, 205

Jardine, Henry 95, 96
Jessop, William 97, 99, 101, 103, 106
John Gibb & Son of Aberdeen 137, 138, 146, 148
Johnson, Samuel 15, 47, 130
Jura 191

Kaffir 216
Karr, John Seaton 125
Keir, Harriet 184
Kennedy, Danny 219, 220
Kennet and Avon Canal 9, 60, 103
Kerr, Margaret 148
Kilduskland 119
Kilmahumaig 72, 166, 213, 223
Kilmartin 23, 45, 55, 56, 194, 195, 221
Kilmory 121, 184, 188
King Edward 197
Kinlochleven 195, 202
Knapdale 18, 23, 116, 169, 194, 195
Knox, John 5, 6, 10, 17, 108

Lachlan of MacLachlan 200, 203
Lake Ladoga 34
Lamlash 67, 68
Lamont, Coll (of Moneydrain) 11, 42, 43, 225
Lamont, Duncan 197
Lancaster 67
Lancaster Canal 9, 23, 39

INDEX

Lang, Revd John Duncan 155
Langlands, Alexander 40
Langlands, George 40, 42, 43–4, 45–6, 108
Languedoc 69, 70
Leckie, Joseph MP 213
Leith 9, 30, 39, 64, 75, 83, 89, 98, 100
Linnet 11, 182–3, 185, 187, 211, 214
Liverpool 26, 67
Lloyd's of London 66
Loch Awe 45, 46
Loch Crinan 9, 11, 17, 19, 31, 37, 57, 161, 193
Loch Fyne 1, 2, 4, 6, 10, 11, 17, 31, 34, 41, 47, 57, 122, 129, 130, 161, 174, 215
Loch Gilp 3, 9, 17, 19, 31, 59, 172, 184, 192, 193, 224
Loch Na Feolin 106, 107
Lochanadd 107, 165
Lochgair 57
Lochgilphead 25, 33, 42, 45, 57, 140, 161, 162, 172, 174, 175, 184, 192, 194, 205, 223
Lochranza 68
London 2, 5, 6, 9, 13, 16, 20, 28, 30, 38, 47, 55, 56, 64, 66, 70, 75, 107, 126, 139, 151, 173, 175, 176, 215
Lorne, George, Marquis of 33, 53, 155, 157–8, 159
Lorne, John, Marquis of 160

M'Thamais, Duncan 36
Macarthur & Co. 63
MacBrain, John 44
MacBrayne, David 182, 186, 187, 211
MacDowall, Charles 'Crichan' 19
Mackenzie, Revd Mr Alexander 116, 169
MacNee, Peter 186
MacNeill, John of Gigha 33, 41, 44, 49, 74, 183–4
Macneill, Duncan MP 171
Macquisten, Frederick Alexander MP 209, 210–11
MacTavish of Dunardry, Dugald (& 'Dougald') 3, 4, 221
MacTavish of Dunardry, Lachlan 11, 25, 31–2, 33, 35–7, 38–45, 65, 225

MacTavish, Captain Duncan 44, 45
Magnus Barefoot 17
Maid of Perth 181
Malcolm, Neill, MP (13th of Poltalloch) 126, 127, 131, 132, 133, 142, 145, 146, 162, 171
Malcolm, Neill (11th of Poltalloch) 22, 30, 33, 35, 41, 36, 37, 38, 39, 40, 41, 42, 43, 44, 45, 49, 55, 56, 57, 75, 76, 108, 109, 110, 111, 112, 113, 171
Malcolm, Neill (12th of Poltalloch) 38, 113
Malcolms (of Poltalloch) 11, 31, 37, 112, 185
Malthus, Thomas 180
Maryport 67
Maxwell, James of Aros 31, 32
May, George 175, 177
McArthur, Buckie and Gray 75
McCulloch, J.R. 152
McDougall, John 149
McGibbon, Neil 44
McIntyre, John 149
McLachlan, Captain 90, 91
McLachlan, Margaret 148
McLachlan, Robert of Dunadd 33
McTavish, Simon 37
McVean, Hugh 140
Meikle, Andrew 8
Melville, Henry Dundas, 1st Viscount 105
Messrs Hutcheson and MacBrayne 185
Minsk 67
Moneydrain 43, 49, 225
Morris, William & Lewis 3
Morrison, Herbert 209
Morrison, W. Murray 202
Muir, Paterson and Burns 62
Muirhead & Co. 50
Mull (isle of) 31, 32, 66, 67, 162
Mull of Kintyre (also 'Cantire' and 'Kantire') 4, 6, 8, 18, 25, 28, 29, 66, 90, 144, 162, 168, 182, 192, 195
Munich (exhibition) 194
Munro, Neil 93
Murray, James of Broughton 7
Murray, Lord George Augustus 155

Naples 49

Napoleon Bonaparte 49, 58, 104, 108, 220
Newcastle 198
Newfoundland 67

Oakfield 41, 50, 60, 62, 71, 73, 101, 137, 172, 184
Oban 123, 161–2, 181, 186, 187, 189, 195, 200–1, 211
Ochil Hills 4
Orde, Sir John P. 161
Orkneys 78
Oxford Canal 103

Palmerston, Viscount 1176, 178
Paterson, John 9, 38–9, 47–8, 49, 69–71, 73–6, 78–83–94, 95, 97–102, 108, 119, 121, 124, 143, 169 221
Patten MacDougall, J. of Gallenach 201
Peel, Sir Robert 52
Pitt, William (the Younger) 20
Poltalloch 11, 35, 36, 49, 55, 185
Port Glasgow 65, 122
Portpatrick 119
Prince Edward Island 158

Prospect Farm 112
Pulteney, William MP 33
Purdie, James 214

Rankin, John 140
Rennie, John 8–9, 10, 20, 23, 25, 28, 31, 33, 39, 40–1, 43, 47, 50–2, 59–64, 65, 74, 75, 77–9, 82, 90, 101–4, 115, 119, 121, 144, 190, 198, 199, 219
Reynolds, Joshua 2
Robison, Duncan 98
Rochdale Canal 9
Rothesay 65, 66
Royal Hotel (Grey Gull) 187
Royal Military Canal (Kent) 104
Russia 3, 5, 34

St Petersburg 3, 34
Saltcoats 67
Scapa Flow 203, 205
Schaw, Charles (*see* Cathcart)
Schaw, Marion 7
Scott, Sir Walter 152
Seahawk, HMS 215
Simpson, Thomas 79, 80, 81, 82–3, 85–90, 91, 92–4, 100, 101

Singapore 202
Sir John Wolfe Barry and Partners 200
Skye 67
Smiles, Samuel 16, 20
Smith, Adam 14
Smith, Samuel 128, 131, 136
Smollett, Patrick MP 177
Smollett, Alexander MP 177
South Knapdale 116, 169
Staffa 162
Stephenson, Robert 149, 152
Steuart, Robert 143
Stevenson, Robert 114–15, 116
Stirling 4
Stranraer 65, 67
Sunbeam 181, 218
Swan, Joseph 194

Tarbert 3, 7, 17, 18, 19, 22, 23, 100, 144, 198
Taymouth Castle 159
Taynaliskan 44
Telford, Thomas 10, 33, 77–9, 80–2, 87, 89, 96–7, 99, 100–1, 116–17, 118–19, 123, 128, 131, 133, 137, 143, 144, 151, 219
Thomas, Daniel 98
Thomson and McConnell 129
Thomson, J & G Ltd 182
Thomson, William 124–5, 128–31, 132–9, 142, 145–7, 164–70, 172
Tiree (also Tyree) 30, 66, 67, 156, 157
Tobermory 109, 120, 157
Turbine Steamers Ltd 197
Tyndrum 45

Ullapool 109
Ulverston 67

Victoria and Albert 161–2
Victoria, Queen 10, 158–64, 169, 181, 211, 217–18

Wade, General (previously Marshall) George 16, 22
Walker, James 132, 137, 140, 144, 145, 146, 147–9
Watt, James (engineer) 7–9, 14–15, 16, 17–19, 23, 25, 33–4, 39, 40, 41,

52, 77–8, 88–9 104, 121, 144, 153, 198, 199
Watt, James (senior) 7, 18
Wedgwood organisation 33–4
Wedgwood, Josiah 33, 34
West Indies 26
Western Isles 29, 68, 157, 182, 205
Whitehaven 67
William Hay & Co. 186
Williams, W. MP 176

Williamson, Captain John 197–8
Wollstonecraft, Mary 32
Wordsworth, Dorothy 16, 48, 130
Wordsworth, William 16, 130
Workington 67
Wren, Sir Christopher 9
Wright, James 4

Zulu 216